Home
FOR
Christmas

Home
FOR
Christmas

MELINDA RATHJEN, EDITOR

IDEALS PUBLICATIONS
NASHVILLE, TENNESSEE

An Ideals Treasury of Christmas
ISBN-13: 978-0-8249-5910-4

Published by Ideals Publications
A Guideposts Company
Nashville, Tennessee
www.idealsbooks.com

Previously published as *Home for Christmas*, copyright © 2008

Printed and bound in the USA

Publisher, Peggy Schaefer
Editor, Melinda Rathjen
Designers, Marisa Jackson and Eve DeGrie
Permissions Editor, Patsy Jay
Songs arranged and set by Dick Torrans

ACKNOWLEDGMENTS

BEDFORD, FAITH ANDREWS. "The Last Day of Christmas" from *Country Living*, December 2003. Used by permission of Faith Andrews Bedford. BOONE, JOY BALE. "The Proof of Mother's Pudding" from *A Kentucky Christmas*. The University Press of Kentucky, 2003. CALVERT, CATHERINE. "Wrapping Up a Memory" from *The Quiet Center*. Edited by Katherine Ball Ross. Published by the Hearst Corporation, 1997 and "Sugar Santa" from *Victoria* Magazine, Dec. 2001. Published by the Hearst Corporation. CONGER, LESLEY. "Tree Dressing." Excerpted from "January" from *Love and Peanut Butter*. Copyright © 1961 by Lesley Conger. Published by W. W. Norton & Company, Inc. FISHER, AILEEN. "Christmas Secrets" from *Out in the Dark and Daylight* by Aileen Fisher. Copyright © 1980 by the author. Used by permission of Marian Reiner on behalf of the Boulder Public Library Foundation, Inc. HARDIN, DOROTHY. "Christmas in the Little Town" from *Good Old Days Presents: Hometown Memories*, edited by Ken and Janice Tate. Copyright © 1999 by House of White Birches. Used by permission of DRG Publishing. JAQUES, EDNA. "Christmas Dinner" from *Uphill All the Way* by Edna Jaques and "Skating Pond." Used by permission of Louise Bonnell. KOETZ, MARILYN. "The Gift" from *Christmas: An Annual Treasury*, Vol. 65. Published by Augsburg Fortress, 1995. Used by permission of the author. LEIMBACH, PATRICIA PENTON. "The Stars Are Brightly Shining" from *Harvest of Bittersweet*. Copyright © 1987 by Patricia Penton Leimbach. Published by Harper & Row. Used by permission of the author. L'ENGLE, MADELEINE. "A Crosswicks Kind of Christmas" from *The Quiet Center*, edited by Katherine Ball Ross, © 1997 by the Hearst Corp. Material previously appeared in *Victoria* Magazine. LOGAN, BEN. "Visions of a Tree" and "Wrapping and Unwrapping" from *Christmas Remembered*. Copyright © 1997 by Ben Logan. Used by permission of Frances Collin, Literary Agent. MARSHALL, HELEN LOWRIE. "Tradition Time" from *Christmas Joys*, edited by Joan Winmill Brown, Doubleday, 1982. McGUIRE, ELAINE YOUNG. "Tennessee Celebrations" from *The Rocking Chair Reader: Family Gatherings*, edited by Helen Kay Polaski. Published 2005 by F+W Publications, Inc., Adams Media. All rights reserved. Used by permission. MOLE, JOHN. "The Waiting Game" from *The Young Oxford Book of Christmas Poems*. Oxford University Press, 2000. Used by permission of John Mole. REDMAN, ELIZABETH. "Christmas in a Nutshell" from *Victoria* Magazine, Dec. 2000. SCHAEFFER, EDITH. "The Importance of Traditions" from *What Is a Family*. Copyright © 1975 by Edith Schaeffer. Published by Fleming H. Revell Co. Used by permission of the Baker Book House Company. SMITH, LILLIAN. "The Christmas Kitchen" from *Memory of a Large Christmas* by Lillian Smith. Copyright © 1962 by the author. Used by permission of W. W. Norton & Company, Inc. TOTH, SUSAN ALLEN. "The Cut-Glass Christmas" from *How to Prepare for Your High-School Reunion* by Susan Allen Toth. Copyright © 1988 by the author. Published by Ballantine Publishing Group, Random House, Inc. Used by permission of The Friedrich Agency. WOODHULL, RITA. "The Christmas Eve Feast Continues" from *The Christmases We Used to Know*. Published by Reminisce Books. Copyright © 1996 Reiman Publications. OUR THANKS TO THE FOLLOWING AUTHORS OR THEIR HEIRS, some of whom we may have been unable to locate: Zelma Bomar, Gladys Billings Bratton, Danielle Brown, Lucille McBroom Crumley, Joan Donaldson, Katherine Edelman, George L. Ehrman, Jessee Fleming, Donna Arlynn Frisinger, Earle J. Grant, Nelle Hardgrove, Bernice C. Heisler, Arlene C. Hercher, Linda Heuring, Burton Hillis, Elizabeth A. Hobsek, Kay Hoffman, Mildred L. Jarrell, Fairy Walker Lane, Vicky A. Luong, Alice Leedy Mason, Marion McClintock, Patricia Rose Mongeau, Virginia Blanck Moore, Lolita Pinney, Mary E. Rathfon, Alice Kenelly Roberts, Margaret L. Rorke, Garnett Ann Schultz, Ann Silva, Mark Sparkman, L. June Stevenson, Ken Studebaker, Ruth H. Underhill, Carice Williams, and Elisabeth Weaver Winstead.

Every effort has been made to establish ownership and use of each selection in this book. If contacted, the publisher will be pleased to rectify any inadvertent errors or omissions in subsequent editions.

ADDITIONAL ART CREDITS

Cover painting, *Christmas Door 2* by Lesley Hammett. Image © DDFA.com; pages 2–3, *Christmas Door 1* by Lesley Hammett. Image © DDFA.com; pages 6–7, *Christmas Trees* by Janet Lawson. Image © DDFA.com; pages 26–27, *Christmas Welcome* by Lesley Hammett. Image © DDFA.com; pages 48–49, *Country House* by Janet Lawson. Image © DDFA.com; pages 78–79, *Christmas Tea* by Lesley Hammett. Image © DDFA.com; pages 110–111, *Xmas Morning* by Lesley Hammett. Image © DDFA.com; pages 138–139, *Cottages & Trees* by Janet Lawson. Image © DDFA.com.; images on pages 10, 51, 91, 97, 99, 109, and 141 from Getty Images, Inc.; holly illustration on cover and pages 1 and 2 © iStockphoto/Dan Tero; background snowflake pattern © iStockphoto/Olga Telnova; striped background © iStockphoto/Donna Franklin; gift tag image © iStockphoto/Nilgun Bostanci; red bow image, © iStockphoto/Boris Yankov; Holly image, pages 6, 9, 17, 25, 26, 30, 32, 41, 43, 48, 55, 63, 69, 73, 77, 78, 83, 89, 90, 99, 103, 107, 110, 113, 119, 127, 133, 138, 149, 155, 159, © iStockphoto/Jan Rysavy; holly sprig image, pages 5, 11, 14, 19, 29, 37, 44, 50, 57, 67, 75, 95, 105, 115, 121, 129, 137, 143, 151, 158, © iStockphoto/Judson Lane; holly, pages 8, 38, 64, 76, 92, 102, 108, 130, 154, © iStockphoto/Lisa Thornberg; holly and pine cones, pages 30, 42, 52, 68, 80, 106, 124, 144, © iStockphoto/Chen Chun Wu; holly and pine cones, pages 16, 86, 116, © iStockphoto/James Knighten; holly and ribbon, pages 22, 60, 72, 90, 96, 112, 140, © iStockphoto/Hannah Gleg.

Contents

WELCOME

Home

—m—

The snow is white and glistening;

The stars shine bright above.

I'm going home for Christmas,

Home to those I love.

GLADYS BILLINGS BRATTON

HOME FOR CHRISTMAS

LINDA HEURING

Being home for Christmas isn't as much fun as coming home for Christmas. For nineteen of the last twenty-one years, I've traveled over lots of rivers and through dozens of woods to arrive home for the holidays.

Every few years, there was a car a little less likely to break down on the road, a new set of highways from which to view deer at daybreak, or a new speed trap to remind us that the police also worked in the wee hours of the morning.

I've brought a husband, a baby, and at least one dog, all settling into my parents' house for the long winter's nap on Christmas Eve. Santa found us there no matter what state was listed on our driver's licenses.

> *GOING HOME MEANT ENTERING . . . A PLACE WHERE I COULD BE A KID AGAIN, MILES FROM . . . MY GROWN-UP RESPONSIBILITIES.*

Our car was laden with baked goods and candy that were more expensive than those from any specialty store, because the phone company, not the grocer, reaped the profits from my culinary attempts. The divinity took four long-distance calls to my mother, one of which resulted from invariably losing the recipe from one year to the next. I would call to find out whether I was supposed to use evaporated or condensed milk in the bonbons and again to find out the amount of peanut butter in the cookie recipe.

There were also calls to discuss presents when we were sure that certain parties were not listening in on the extension. There were the last-minute messages to let my parents know what time we were leaving, and there were calls en route if the weather was particularly bad and we knew they'd be worried.

With the help of a book light or the opened glove compartment, cross-stitched napkins—and more than one afghan—were finished in the car on the drive, but for the most part, the drive signaled the beginning of vacation. It was Christmas.

Bursting into my mother's kitchen while carrying a sleeping child or shepherding a barking dog, we'd see every available inch covered with her own holiday baking—the sugar cookies with sour-cream icing, the divinity with nuts on top, the rum balls, and the buckeyes. We'd have to move containers of chocolate chip cookies to make room for the sandwiches she'd fix as someone's nonstop talking steamed up the windows.

We'd get our son to bed and keep my parents up way too late listening to music, catching up on the news, shaking presents, and eating.

Time was suspended. Work didn't exist. At home, I'd receive calls from the office, but here it was quiet. All calls were from cousins or brothers. Work was putting the decals on a fighter plane, untangling the controller wire on a video game, or opening my eyes after staying up all night with my brothers and their wives.

For the most part, Christmas was part of a time warp. Going home meant entering a twilight zone of sorts, a place where I could be a kid again, miles from my own house, my job, and my grown-up responsibilities. Oh sure, I packed the briefcase of work I couldn't leave behind, but I carried it up to my old room, where it remained until the trip back home.

Living near home for the first time as an adult

has put a crimp in my Christmas. Just spending the day with my family isn't quite the same. I miss the anticipation of the trip. My nephews and niece won't have grown too much since I saw them last; and when the day's over, I won't be headed up the stairs to my old room to take a nap.

Oh, I guess I could take the long route to my parents' house, but even the long way is less than a mile. I suppose we could spend the night there, but it doesn't make sense to make all that extra work for my mom when our own beds are just blocks away.

I'm not sorry to be home, just sorry that I can't freeze time and make Christmas last a little longer before I have to go back to my side of town and become an adult again.

Homeward Bound

Virginia Blanck Moore

My heart is homeward bound these days
Because it's Christmastime.
When I see windows gaily decked
And hear the carols chime,
When I meet parcel-laden folks
Returning smiles with smiles,
My heart goes winging straight across
The intervening miles

To home, to family, and to friends
That childhood days made dear,
To hometown streets where passersby
Greet one with welcoming cheer.
Though years go by, and decades too,
Still I have always found
When Christmastime makes its approach
My heart is homeward bound.

Home for Christmas

Gladys Billings Bratton

Away from busy sights and sounds,
I take the road toward home,
Back to the hills and the valleys,
Back where I loved to roam.

The snow is white and glistening;
The stars shine bright above.
I'm going home for Christmas,
Home to those I love.

The folks will be there waiting
With a smile and open arms;

I'll find warmth and laughter there,
The wealth of homey charms.

There'll be a Christmas tree in the window
As friends and neighbors gather round
To sing the songs of Christmas,
And joy shall there abound.

The road seems long and winding,
But there's happiness at the end;
For I'm going home for Christmas,
And home is round the bend.

Here We Come A-Caroling

TRADITIONAL ENGLISH | TRADITIONAL ENGLISH

joy come to you, and to your car - ol

too, and God bless you and send you a

hap - py New Year, and God send you a

hap - py New Year.

Christmas at Home

JESSEE FLEMING

This is a Christmas story
Of a special place I know:
The home that I was raised in,
The home that I love so.

The house is all made ready
For the coming special day;
There's fruit and nuts in every bowl
And cookies bright and gay.

There's turkey in the oven
With the trimmings setting round;
There's fruitcake on the table
And candy by the pound.

We gather round the special place
To trim the Christmas tree;
We place the angel on the top
To bless this family.

The sound of music fills the air;
The Christmas carols play;
We all join hands and sing along
To welcome Christmas Day.

This special home will always be
The dearest place I know;
It's always filled with warmth and love
And has a special glow.

Bristol, New Hampshire. Photograph © William H. Johnson

CHRISTMAS IN A NUTSHELL

ELIZABETH REDMAN

*T*he scent of lilacs and Persian Yellow roses, ponderosa pines in the summer heat, a clump of hollyhocks—all of these trigger memories of childhood. But the one thing that brings back the earliest and most vivid memories of all is a dried litchi shell. Strange as it may seem, this small brown object evokes my childhood home—the apartment house at 19 East Phoenix Avenue—as nothing else can. I have never known why my mother kept it, but in doing so she gave me a talisman of the past. When I hold it, the memories return as if by magic, and I am back in the Flagstaff, Arizona, of my youth.

The litchi came to our home at Christmastime, via the Chinese laundry down the street. Every year, Wong June would send his children out with small holiday gifts for his steady customers, as did many business owners. . . . Wong June's tokens of appreciation had an exotic air: a small tin of tea, a glazed green jar of candied ginger, a box of litchis. Being a world-class accumulator, my mother held on to one of the latter until it dried into a hollow shell that rested in a small china bowl for several years, then found a home in her secretary desk. I often opened the small drawer where the litchi was stored and took it out, savoring the rough texture of the shell with its patterned bumps and its faint, curious smell.

*H*OW DO YOU EXPLAIN AN ATTACHMENT TO SOMETHING THAT BRINGS BACK YOUR CHILDHOOD?

With each of several household moves, the litchi was packed and brought along. When the time came to transplant my mother's possessions from the Arizona desert to the high country of Montana, the litchi made the move too, although many more obviously valuable items wound up at antiques shops or the Salvation Army. I couldn't explain why I insisted on keeping the little nut.

But then, how do you explain an attachment to something that brings back your childhood? And not just memories of the Chinese laundry, with its smell of clean linens being ironed or the embroidered silk pictures on the wall of the

Wongs' living quarters. The litchi brings back the sandstone apartment house with the low stone wall I liked to walk on, the hollyhocks growing in the vacant lot next door, the tiny cake decorations of sugar birds and flowers that I carefully kept for years on the top shelf of my toy cupboard. . . . These and other memories come from the litchi like smoke from a genie's lamp. Appropriately, some of the most vivid are of Christmas.

Flagstaff was a Christmas-card town, surrounded by tall pines often covered with snow and framed by clear blue skies. When houses started displaying wreaths on doors and trees in windows around mid-December, my walk to school became a dawdle. At school, art class was devoted to making paper chains and presents for our parents, music for practicing Christmas carols for our annual program. On one weekend each holiday season, my mother would take me to town to pick out a present for my teacher. I would choose between a handkerchief and a box of stationery, both within the guidelines of being useful and modestly priced. Afterward, we would visit Santa's workshop at the J.C. Penney store and look at other store window displays, finishing our tour with a fresh doughnut from the bakery on Front Street.

Baking at home began with traditional springerle. For most people, the scent that says Christmas is of evergreens and spices, but for me it is the faint licorice smell of anise from the molded cookies left out to dry overnight before baking. Later in the month my mother baked date bars, Mexican wedding cakes, chocolate pinwheels, and butter cookies to give as gifts to friends. Our share was augmented by a parcel from Aunt Clara's bak-

ery in Las Vegas, New Mexico, containing lebkuchen and her justly famous fruitcake. My father's role in the Christmas preparations was . . . putting up the Christmas tree. All of our ornaments were lovely handblown glass from Germany—birds with long tails, Santas, a bell with a tiny glass clapper, a horn you could blow, a "lucky" red-and-white mushroom.

The litchi from a long-ago Christmas now reposes in a small Hopi bowl in my mother's bookcase, among other mementos of her life in New Mexico and Arizona. And should I ever move again, it will come along, small and apparently insignificant, but the key that unlocks a part of my childhood.

Photograph © Jessie Walker

Homecoming

MARION MCCLINTOCK

Bring the star, the lights, the tinsel;

Have the crèche assembled here.

To the spicy suet pudding

Add a bit of Christmas cheer.

Decorating ginger cookies,

This day merges with the past,

Carilloned with loving greetings,

Holding blessed memories fast.

Soon the rooms will ring with laughter;

Soon the hearth will beckon near.

Carolers outside the window

Find a waiting welcome here.

Sleepy children will be bedded;

Conversations soft and low;

Through the year with each returning,

Love has cast its golden glow.

They'll Be Home for Christmas

NELLE HARDGROVE

Jingle bells and tinsel

And trimmings tucked away

Are coming from their

    wrappings

To grace the holiday.

Cookies in the making

And presents ten feet tall,

Songs to sing and bells to ring

And Christmas cheer for all.

Dreams and hopes and wishes

Will all be coming true.

But, best of all,

The ones you love

Are coming home to you!

Bacon-Wrapped Smokies

1   14-ounce package beef cocktail wieners
1   pound sliced bacon, cut into thirds
¾   cup brown sugar, or to taste

Preheat oven to 325°F. Wrap each cocktail wiener with a piece of bacon and secure with a toothpick (it is easier to wrap the wieners with cold bacon). Place on a large baking sheet. Sprinkle brown sugar generously all over. Bake for 40 minutes or until the sugar is bubbly. To serve, place the wieners in a slow cooker on the low setting.

Raspberry Cheese Spread

4   ounces cream cheese, softened
1   cup mayonnaise
2   cups shredded mozzarella cheese
8   ounces Cheddar cheese, shredded

3   green onions, finely chopped
1   cup chopped pecans
¼   cup seedless raspberry preserves
  Assorted crackers

Line a 9-inch round baking dish with plastic wrap; set aside. In a small bowl, beat the cream cheese and mayonnaise until blended. Beat in cheeses and onions. Stir in pecans. Spread mixture into prepared dish; cover with plastic wrap and refrigerate until set, about 1 hour.

Invert onto serving plate and remove plastic wrap. Spread with preserves. Serve with crackers.

Spiced Party Mix

2 large egg whites
1½ teaspoons Worcestershire sauce
¼ cup granulated sugar
2 tablespoons sweet paprika
1½ teaspoons cayenne
9 cups freshly popped unsalted popcorn

2 cups miniature pretzels
1½ cups salted roasted peanuts
1½ cups pecans, toasted
1½ cups whole almonds, toasted
1½ cups salted roasted cashews
Salt

Preheat oven to 325°F. In a large bowl, whisk together egg whites, Worcestershire sauce, sugar, paprika, and cayenne. Add popcorn, pretzels, and nuts. Toss until thoroughly coated and salt to taste. Spread evenly in 2 large, greased baking pans. Bake in upper and lower thirds of oven, switching positions of pans halfway through baking, until coating is crisp, about 20 minutes total.

Spread mixture on 2 large sheets of parchment paper or oiled foil and cool completely.

Cheesy Baked Artichoke Dip

1 14-ounce can artichoke hearts, drained and chopped
1 cup mayonnaise
1½ cups grated Parmesan cheese, divided
1½ cups shredded mozzarella cheese, divided
½ teaspoon garlic powder

Salt and black pepper
Dash of hot sauce
Dash of Worcestershire sauce
1 tablespoon butter
½ cup minced yellow onion
French bread or tortilla chips

Preheat oven to 375°F. In a large bowl, mix together artichoke hearts, mayonnaise, 1 cup Parmesan, 1 cup mozzarella, garlic powder, salt, pepper, hot sauce, and Worcestershire sauce; set aside. In a small skillet over medium heat, melt the butter. Add the onion and sauté 8 to 10 minutes or until light golden brown. Remove from heat and let cool slightly. Pour into artichoke mixture; mix well. Pour into baking or casserole dish. Top with remaining cheese. Bake 30 to 40 minutes or until golden brown and bubbly. Serve warm with toasted French bread or tortilla chips.

A Crosswicks Kind of Christmas

Madeleine L'Engle

Christmas, that time of light coming in the midst of the darkest nights of the year, has always been important to me. When I was a little girl, I lived in New York City; and one of my loveliest memories is of searching for all the trees in the city that were decorated with colored lights, something that once more captures my imagination now that I am back in the city. But when my children were growing up, we lived in a dairy village in Connecticut where the nights were usually illumed with nothing but stars. The traditions of my girlhood—I was an only child and Christmases were often spent with just my parents—didn't quite work in an old farmhouse like Crosswicks, filled with three children and lots of hustle and bustle. So my husband, Hugh, and I set about inventing our own ways of celebrating both Christmas and the other special times that knit a family together.

> **EVERYTHING NEW THAT WE DID QUICKLY BECAME A HOLIDAY FIXTURE.**

My birthday comes as Advent begins, so those weeks before Christmas are the first weeks in my personal New Year, as well as the church's. . . . One year I found a cardboard cutout of about twenty small elves dancing, and I hung it in the kitchen windows. That quickly became a tradition. So did taking an old coat hanger and some fishing thread and a dozen decorations to make a mobile that swung from the ceiling and dangled over the kitchen counter as we rolled cookie dough. When I found brightly colored cutouts of Santa Claus with his sleigh and reindeer, they went up the front staircase, so that we had to be careful not to knock them off as we held on to the banister. Everything new that we did quickly became a holiday fixture. We added and added and only subtracted when something fell apart.

One of the greatest of all the great days of Advent was driving five miles to the house of a retired Congregational minister and his wife to cut down our Yuletide tree and have high tea, a real experience for my children. In our village, there wasn't much chance for a plain cup of tea in the afternoon, much

Photograph © Jessie Walker

less one spiced with cinnamon and cloves and accompanied by soft-boiled egg, sandwiches, and pound cake. Tea, however, was only a prelude to the main event. Warmed to our toes, we were given a saw and rope, and we headed to the woods to choose just the right tree. Row after row of pines

$\mathcal{W}$HEN I WAS A CHILD, MY PARENTS DECORATED THE TREE TOGETHER ON CHRISTMAS EVE. . . .

had been planted many years ago by this wonderful couple in anticipation of Christmas visits from children just like my three. We all took a turn sawing, and then we tied the tree's branches together and dragged it back to the car.

When I was a child, my parents decorated the tree together on Christmas Eve, and I never saw it until the next morning. I'm not sure how my husband and I started Christmas-tree Sunday, with the children helping with the decorating, but that became our tradition. We sang carols and had eggnog round the piano. The unbreakable decorations were given to the little ones to put on the bottom branches, a tradition that evolved not only for the sake of eager little fingers, but for the cats (who in my memory are always kittens) and for the dogs, who were always overinterested in what was going on.

For several years we included the celebration of Hanukkah, another feast of light at the darkest time of the year. What I loved most about Hanukkah was

that the rejoicing was not so much for the victorious battle, but for the lamp in the temple that had oil enough for only a day, yet burned brightly for seven days and nights.

Since I was the choir director of our little church, the Christmas Eve service was a big part of our lives, as well as decorating the church with greens and many candles. It seemed to me that we all sang better by candlelight than by electric light, and I don't think this was only my imagination.

Reading aloud at bedtime was an every-night tradition, but on Christmas Eve after church, my husband would read The Night Before Christmas and the Christmas story from St. Luke, while we all sipped hot cocoa. Then the children went up to bed, being warned about not waking us up too early in the morning.

We gave each of them a present to open in their rooms so that Hugh and I had a fighting chance of getting some sleep. We needed it. Christmas was a very busy time at the country store we ran—we usually had a number of people's turkeys thawing, countless orders only just filled—and the wee hours of Christmas Eve were traditionally spent putting together a bicycle or a doll's house or a train set. Neither of us was born with carpentry skills. We read the directions, but they were usually wrong. Oh, for a magic wand to make all those little pieces go together!

In the early days we had Christmas dinner at noon, but no one liked it. The idea of sleeping with the newspaper over one's face all afternoon wasn't appealing. So we settled on brunch and then dinner, which, as a concession, was planned to be an hour and a half early. But somehow we always ended

up eating at the regular time anyway. Over the years we had innovations—one Christmas it was a goose, another a suckling pig—but finally we settled on the more traditional turkey. Actually two turkeys, twenty-five pounds each, one with bread-and-herb stuffing, the other dressed more experimentally with cornbread or oysters or chestnuts or apricots. Because my mother was a Southerner, we always had rice and gravy. We gave up the candied sweet potatoes a good many years ago. Delicious though they were, I finally realized nobody ate them. But the creamed onions, the leeks and carrots, cut lengthwise and braised, persist to this day. Dessert? I am not a dessert cook! Sometimes there's a plum pudding to flame, sometimes a pie someone has baked and brought. After our regular meal, we really aren't interested in desserts.

Families grow up, change. Traditions change. We can't hold on to them too tightly or they become rigid. Wait. New traditions will happen.

Today Christmas comes to Crosswicks with an influx of family and friends, old and new. Breakfast is cooked by my son, who keeps an eye on the modern concerns of cholesterol. The unbreakable ornaments are still hung on the bottom branches. Are the children old enough for us to assemble the train set? Not quite. Let's wait. Next year, perhaps, that will be yet another Christmas tradition.

OVER THE
Hills
AND
AROUND TOWN

————— ∞ —————

Sing hey! Sing hey! For Christmas Day!

Twine mistletoe and holly.

For a friendship glows in winter snows,

And so let's all be jolly!

AUTHOR UNKNOWN

Milford, New Hampshire. Photograph © William H. Johnson

Winter Peace

RUTH H. UNDERHILL

Softly the snowflakes drifted down,
Quietly blanketing our peaceful town;
Each tree adorned in shimmering white
Beneath the moon of silvery light.

The rows of houses along each street
Are nestled securely in darkness deep;
The smoke from chimneys in curly form
Assures of people safe and warm.

In the distance, a tinkle of silvery bells
As a sleigh skims over the hills;
The gong of a church bell in steeple high
Echoes across the snow-darkened sky.

A portrait of nature in a white wonderland,
Perfectly painted by God's great hand.
A snow-capped village 'neath silvery glow:
A magical scene on Earth below.

Sublime Landscape

ELIZABETH A. HOBSEK

It's still tonight; each lamplight
Casts a haloed glow.
The moon on high, through wisps of white,
Transforms the scene below.

Candles grace one windowpane;
The snow that frosts our yard
Glints from silver to gold again—
Like a foiled Christmas card.

Crystals flash on the back pond
As skaters swirl, then briskly glide
To the warming house beyond,
And a blazing stove inside.

It's midnight; vast starlight
Shimmers over the eaves.
What a wrap of jeweled delight
Father Winter weaves!

CHRISTMAS IN THE LITTLE TOWN

DOROTHY HARDIN

Christmas wasn't a big production number in the 1930s. The onslaught of high-pressure advertising was still light-years away, so contact with the outside world was by word of mouth, radio, and the Montgomery catalog. Our hometown was, I suppose, like any other during the Depression—licking its collective wounds and hoping for better days ahead. Neighbors clung to one another and offered help when needed. At our house there was no woe-is-me attitude, and if we were deprived, we didn't know it. Humor and laughter prevailed. We were, after all, together.

Our little town—where my father was born in 1886—resembled a pastoral scene set to music. Alfalfa fields as green as emeralds skirted the landscape. Hay and pastureland reached out to touch the foothills. Dairy cows dotted the valley floor.

CHRISTMAS TRIGGERS FLASHBACKS TO THE CHILD IN ALL OF US, SPICED WITH THE TENDERNESS AND LONGING OF ALL OUR YESTERDAYS.

The westbound passenger train stopped for passengers every morning at 8:20. At high noon the fire siren signaled it was time to knock off for lunch. Christmas shopping was simple then. There was little money to spend, and choices were few. Local merchants knew each customer's name and the ages of all the children. My yearly pilgrimage to Pete Christesen's store to buy my father a bandanna was a case in point. The few coins held tightly in my sweaty palm just barely covered the cost of one handkerchief, and choosing between a red one and a blue one seemed impossible. Sensing a panic attack in the making, Pete made the decision for me.

"Why not get the red one this time? I'll save the blue one for you when you come back next year."

I genuinely believed him! Christesen's store at that precise moment acquired a customer for life.

Kolln Hardware was another kid-pleaser. Browsing was welcomed even in the china department at the far corner of the cavernous store. The wooden floors creaked and groaned, and we children tiptoed rather than disturb the bookkeeper, who was adding up figures in her glass enclosure.

It was at Kolln's that my brother found the first gift he could afford for our mother: a potbellied teapot of cobalt blue, trimmed in gold and bearing the likeness of a sumo wrestler. Sporting a cherubic face with dimpled chin, the warrior was most impressive. One muscular arm served as a handle, the other a spout. It became a treasured conversation piece used only for special occasions, and after more than half a century, the sumo teapot is still in trim condition without a chip or crack to mar its surface.

Merchants lining the avenue of memory called Main Street offered little in the way of holiday decorations to dazzle the eye at Christmastime. Just a swag of glitter to outline the curve of a store front, a touch of fresh holly, perhaps a gaily lit tree or two—these were frugal times.

The first inkling that Christmas was beginning to weave its magic was the arrival of a package from our maiden aunt, Annie. The package always contained a new sweater for each of us.

The closer it came to the holidays, the sweeter our house became. Mom insisted she was a plain cook, but we knew better. Her fruitcake was guaranteed to turn any fruitcake-hater into a true believer.

Tree trimming was a job reserved for the younger generation. We quickly tired of draping strands of tinsel in a perfect parade over each branch and instead wadded the strands into small balls and let them fall where they would. Ever the perfectionist, our big sister sneaked back into the living room during the dead of night and redid the tree to her own liking.

Christmas triggers flashbacks to the child in all of us, spiced with the tenderness and longing of all our yesterdays. My grandchild, eyes brimming with wonder, asks me, "What was Christmas like in the old days, Grandma?" I wince and look around to ask someone of the older generation and then realize I'm it! I try my best to explain to her that Christmas never changes and is neither old nor new. Christmas is love. May yours be a joyful one.

Peacham, Vermont. Photograph © William H. Johnson

Last-Minute Shopping

EARLE J. GRANT

Our village is cloaked
In sparkling white snow;
Through crystalline air
Sweet old carols flow.

There is candlelight
Against windowpanes
Of quaint cottages
And snow-covered lanes.

Rainbow-colored lights
Trim the Christmas trees
That stand like flowers
In the spruce-scented breeze.

A few late shoppers
Hurry to-and-fro,
With their faces shining
Beneath the moon's glow.

It seems that heaven
And earth somehow meet
When Christmas Eve comes
To our village street.

Leavenworth, Washington. Photograph © Terry Donnelly/Donnelly Austin Photography

Jingle Bells

James Lord Pierpont

Photograph © Nancy Matthews

Christmas Sled

AUTHOR UNKNOWN

Oh, for the winters that used to be!
The winters that only a boy may see!
Rich with the snowflakes' rush and swirl;
Keen as a diamond, pure as a pearl;
Brimming with healthful, rollicking fun;
Sweet with their rest when the play
    was done,
With kindly revels each day decreed,
And a Christmas sled for the royal steed.

Down from the crest with shrill hurray!
Clear the track, there! Out of the way!
Scarcely touching the path beneath,
Scarce admitting of breath to breathe,
Dashing along, with leap and swerve,
Over the crossing, round the curve.
Talk of your flying machines! Instead,
Give me the swoop of that
    Christmas sled.

Coasting Time

ZELMA BOMAR

On sleds we coasted down the hill,
Laughing if we took a spill;
We were always glad to know
When the weatherman said snow.

Happy shouts rang on the air
As sleds were gliding everywhere;
Climb the hill, then down you go

Over the white and sparkling snow.
Trudging up the slippery slope,
Pulling sleds by lengths of rope,
When at last we reached the crest,
Paused a while to sit and rest.

Snow and sleds, plus girls and boys,
Gladly welcomed winter's joys.

A Christmas Eve Ride

MARK SPARKMAN

We lived in the small, cozy town of Bellwood, Pennsylvania. In the seven years of my childhood that we lived there, I can't remember not having snow during the Christmas season. I was about nine or ten years old at the time, and my older brother and I had received our snow sled from Santa the previous year. It was a "Flexible-Flyer," no less—the gold standard by which children's snow sleds of the day were measured. It was our most prized possession of wintertime.

The weeks preceeding Christmas were filled with the usual flurry of activities and anticipation. The school Christmas assembly punctuated the final day and signaled the long-awaited beginning of Christmas vacation. This meant we were completely free to spend our days sled-riding down our favorite slope until too cold and too tired to do it any more. We would go home, thaw, and dry out over some hot chocolate and a sandwich, only to go right back outside for more.

> WE WENT OUT ONTO THE FROZEN PORCH, GRABBED THE NEVER-FAILING FLEXIBLE-FLYER . . . AND BEGAN OUR ASCENT TO BAKER'S HILL.

It was actually a street that was usually, though not always, blocked off when a heavy snow came; and kids from neighborhoods near and far would converge on it for the sole purpose of sledding. Even when it wasn't blocked off, traffic seldom ventured up or down that street. Though not because it was steep so much, I think, as out of respect for the children using it as their snow-covered playground. At least it seemed that way, and Bellwood seemed like that kind of town.

Among the neighborhood kids, it was always referred to as Baker's Hill. We never really knew why, but my little mind speculated that it might have been named after some courageous guy that had died in a wild and spectacular sled-riding accident. I envisioned it to be something akin to the skier we saw on TV

Brookville, Pennsylvania. Photograph © age fotostock/SuperStock

pressed on. Using what salespersons now call "assumptive close," a day or two later I confidently turned to Mom and asked, "What day are we going sled-riding?"

"Oh, I don't know, maybe Christmas Eve after church," Mom said, shooting a less than subtle glance over at Dad that, to me, suggested there was no turning back. The deal was all but sealed!

I don't remember much about that Christmas Eve's church service; most kids probably don't at that age. I am sure my mind was preoccupied not just with the usual images of things to come, but also our sled-riding rendezvous on Baker's Hill that very night! Since the church was only a few blocks from our house, we bundled up and walked to the Christmas Eve service.

As we came out of the church, evening darkness had overtaken the town, and snow was falling. It was one of those slow but consistently falling snows: no wind, just big, soft, fluffy flakes floating straight down and every bit of it sticking to the already packed layer on the streets. Perfect for sled-riding.

The streets all the way home appeared deserted. There was not a moving car or another person in sight. For a while, it seemed like we owned the streets. I remember walking as fast as I could; and every so often, my brother and I would take a big run and go sliding on the slick, snow-packed road.

When we got home, we made a mad dash upstairs to our room to change out of our church

each Sunday tumbling like a rag doll during the opening of ABC's *Wide World of Sports* as announcer Jim McKay would dramatically voice, "The thrill of victory and the agony of defeat!"

It was ideally located, only about one hundred yards from our house; and Mom would watch us out the kitchen window as she stood at the sink doing dishes. In spite of our periodic but persistent pleadings, we could never get Mom and Dad to go sled-riding with us. They typically responded in a way suggesting that they were "too old" for such fun— "Why, we would break our necks!"

With eternal optimism that comes with childhood, we kids never bought these lame excuses. One day I was pleasantly surprised when I saw what appeared to be movement, albeit slight, in a positive direction, when Mom responded with, "Not today, but maybe later, kids."

Perhaps we had pleaded with our parents more than usual, or maybe we had a particularly good amount of snow that year, but not forgetting Mom's slight concession in the ongoing negotiations, I

Goodpasture Bridge in Oregon. Photograph © Dennis Frates

clothes and into our long-johns, two layers of pants, two layers of sweatshirts, coat, gloves, hat, scarf, and boots. Mom dressed my sister, who was only about five years old at the time. We all converged at the front door; and when all hats were in place with ears covered and the last boot had been tied, we went out onto the frozen porch, grabbed the never-failing Flexible-Flyer by the long and frozen-stiff rope handle, and began our ascent to Baker's Hill.

The snow continued to fall like there was no end in sight. The streetlight at the top of the hill illuminated a large halo of falling snow—the same street light I always peered at through the window at night to gage if and how much it was snowing. Once at the top, Dad pulled the sled in position facing down the hill.

Being a former Marine, Dad had a plan—a plan to maximize the ride for his family of five. "For stability," he said, it would all be done according to size. I was eager to see what Dad had in mind. I thought his idea might be based on some little-known training technique he had learned in the Marine Corps. First, he would lay face down on the sled. As he got himself comfortable and in position, the Flexible-Flyer vanished from view beneath his massive torso. Next Mom, face down on top of him. Then it was my brother, two years my senior. Next, it was me, with my little sister clinging to my back at the very top.

Using his feet and hands, Dad slowly and laboriously began inching the heavy, overloaded sled with a teetering tower of five to the edge of the hill. Little by little, we began to move. As we started to slide on our own accord, we all began to intermittently squeal in anticipation. As we gradually increased speed, our squeals turned to screams.

We were off!

Stacked five high, we barreled downhill, swaying from side to side like a sapling pine tree in a windy snowstorm! Each clung tightly as Dad attempted to steer a straight course, but our unintentional swaying made this all but impossible! Our screams grew louder with each teetering sway. At one point, it felt like we had tilted up on only one rudder! As we hit maximum speed, my eyes watered from the cold air and snow hitting my face. The sounds emitting from my mouth were a bizarre hybrid of giggles and screams. The excitement must have temporarily short-circuited the neural pathways between my diaphragm and brain! I couldn't catch my breath.

About halfway down, I was no longer able to make any sound! I had run out of oxygen due to my sister's death grip around my neck!

We all hung on! I could hear Mom squeal, "Oh! Oh! Oh!"

Then, our speed began to gradually wane. We started slowing, and we were all still on! And as we gradually slowed before we came to a complete stop, we all toppled off from the faithful sled and rolled into the snow. Getting up and brushing ourselves off, each of us made loud and enthusiastic declarations of how wild and fun it had all been. I couldn't stop laughing.

I don't remember how many runs down the hill we ultimately did that snowy, Christmas Eve night, but if it had only been that once, it was worth all the waiting in the world. For a nine-year-old boy, it was every bit the "thrill of victory"; and—for a while—time stood still.

GOLDEN MEMORIES OF CHRISTMAS IN COLORADO

ARLENE HERCHER

As we pulled up to the twelve-hundred-square-foot cabin that was to house all thirteen family members plus our many gifts and supplies for the next week, our parents were immediately met with the gleeful shouting of their grandchildren. At fifteen, Jerrid of course was too cool for such demonstrative behavior, but one look into his eyes told the same story as the younger children's shouts. The snow glistened like twinkling gems in the warm Colorado sun, and the sky was deeply blue and dotted with promising snow clouds.

The balance of the day of was spent snowmobiling, building snowmen, sledding, cooking, and eating, then eating some more. Sledding was made far more tolerable by the snowmobile taxi rides to the top of the sledding hills. All of the day's events had taken place on our parents' property. As our families visited together, we mused whether our stay could get any better than our first day already had been. Tori, the next to the oldest grandchild, interjected, "This is like a Christmas in the movies only better because we're really living it!" We all heartily added our agreement. Later that evening, Grandpa announced that the next day would include a trip to the forest for our Christmas tree and an evening car ride to see the herds of elk as they crossed nearby open fields in search of winter food.

> THE PRECIOUSNESS OF THAT FIRST CHRISTMAS DID NOT COME IN WHAT WE RECEIVED IN THE WAY OF GIFTS, BUT IN THE LOVE WE GAVE TO ONE ANOTHER.

After an omelet-and-fried-potato breakfast, we were well fueled for our trip in search of the perfect tree. Grandma, being the insightful person she is, volunteered to stay behind and prepare lunch for our return. As we drove down the highway, the joyful volume of excited voices and the closeness of each squished body caused me to wonder momentarily who the truly smart one of the Meek crew was. That thought quickly vanished as we dashed from tree to tree attempting to convince all the others that the tree of our choice was the best. We finally agreed upon a sixteen-foot-tall pine. It was cut and placed in the truck bed in short order. Caroling our way back to our family home made our return trip pass without incident. We were quick to discover our tree was doomed to the out-of-doors since it was taller and wider than the area available in the cabin. As it turned out, the yard just in front of the cabin made a per-

fect spot. Our masterpiece could even be seen from passersby.

Later in the week we donned cross-country skis and took off across, around, up, and down our parents' property. Two hundred and thirty-eight acres proved more challenge than we were prepared for. The bravest of us, Heinz, Jerrid, and I decided to don our skis one more time. We headed out when the moon rose high above the central valley which extended into the U.S. Forest Service property. Once out on Forest Service property, we received the gift we had hoped for. There, crossing a valley ahead of us, was a large herd of elk. Passing over the open valley one by one, they appeared in ghostly silence. The black of each shadow, the glistening of the snow in the moonlight, and the

excitement we shared will live with me forever. Naturally, we were the envy of our family members. We heard many promises to be joined by others the next Christmas in Colorado.

This will be the third Christmas since our first Christmas in Colorado. We will gather once again. Although Grammy will not be there to share each moment with us, we will bring her there by remembering how special she helped our lives to be. There will be a place for her at the table in memory of the place she holds in each of our hearts. The preciousness of that first Christmas did not come in what we received in the way of gifts, but in the love we gave to one another. . . . We look forward to the joy of another Christmas of love. A Christmas of activity. A Christmas with family.

Photograph © Jessie Walker

Ice Skating

LOLITA PINNEY

The skaters move like restless birds
Beneath dull pewter skies,
Their whirring blades a melody
With chords of joyful cries.

Kaleidoscope of color,
They spin and skim and glide.
Their mittened hands clasped pair by pair,
The wintry winds defied!

Skate right foot first and then the left,
Across black ice, swift flight;
When toes grow cold and fingers numb,
A bonfire lights the night.

Sweet, scalding draughts of chocolate
To drink in twilight style
Reward the swooping skaters
Who pause to rest awhile.

Skating Pond

EDNA JAQUES

They dart about like water bugs
With waving arms and sprawling legs,
Some as graceful as the swans
While others stiff as wooden pegs.
And yet, the fun they have is worth
More than the minted gold of Earth.

The ice is clear as painted glass,
Bordered by heaps of drifted snow;
The winter sky above the trees
Almost as blue as indigo;
A setting lovely as a gem
Set in a vacant lot for them.

They swoop and dip and whirl and dart,
Fall with a thud and slide a bit;
Crawl on all fours like tiny bears,

Yet never seem to tire of it;
But up and at it once again,
Crusted with snow like frozen men.

Their little cheeks are warm and red
Like apples on the rosy side;
Snowsuits of red and green and blue—
The little bodies tucked inside
Are warm as kittens wrapped in wool—
Lovely to look at . . . beautiful.

Here on this vacant lot is heard
Young laughter merry as a lark,
The gay voice of a little girl,
A tiny dog's excited bark,
Where all the bells of heaven chime
Under the spell of wintertime.

Hot Cider Punch

3 cups apple juice	2 cinnamon sticks
2½ cups unsweetened pineapple juice	2 teaspoons whole cloves
2 cups cranberry juice	2 teaspoons ground allspice
¼ cup brown sugar	

In a large saucepan or stockpot over medium-high heat, combine juices and brown sugar. Place cinnamon sticks, cloves, and allspice into a large teaball or cheesecloth bag, and place gently into the juice mixture. Heat for 10 minutes. Remove spices and serve warm. Makes 15 servings.

Creamy Spiced Tea

2½ cups granulated sugar	2 teaspoons ground ginger
1½ cups unsweetened instant tea powder	2 teaspoons ground cinnamon
1 cup nonfat dry milk powder	1 teaspoon ground cloves
1 cup powdered non-dairy creamer	1 teaspoon ground cardamom
1 cup French vanilla–flavored powdered non-dairy creamer	

In a large bowl, combine sugar, tea powder, milk powder, non-dairy creamer, and vanilla-flavored creamer. Stir in the ginger, cinnamon, cloves, and cardamom. In a blender or food processor, blend 1 cup at a time until mixture is the consistency of fine powder. In a teapot or large saucepan, boil water. Pour hot water into mugs. Stir 2 heaping tablespoons of spiced tea mix into each mug. Store remaining mix in an airtight container. Makes 36 servings.

Friendship Tea

1 cup sweetened lemonade powder
1 cup orange-flavored drink mix
½ cup unsweetened instant tea powder

1 teaspoon ground cinnamon
½ teaspoon ground cloves

In a large bowl, combine all ingredients; mix well and store in an airtight container. In a teapot or large saucepan, boil water. Spoon 2 to 3 teaspoons of tea mix into each mug; pour boiling water over mix and stir well. Adjust to taste. Store remaining mix in an airtight container. Makes 40 servings.

Cappuccino Mix

⅔ cup instant coffee granules
1 cup powdered non-dairy creamer
1 cup powdered chocolate drink mix

½ cup granulated sugar
¾ teaspoon ground cinnamon
⅜ teaspoon ground nutmeg

In a food processor, process the instant coffee into a fine powder. In a large bowl, combine the coffee powder with the rest of the ingredients; mix well. In a teapot or large saucepan, boil water. Spoon 3 tablespoons of cappuccino mix into each mug; pour 6 ounces of boiling water over mix and stir well. Makes 16 servings.

Peppermint Hot Cocoa

1 quart milk
1 cup semisweet chocolate chips
¼ cup unsweetened cocoa powder
1 teaspoon vanilla extract

1 teaspoon peppermint extract
Pinch of salt
Whipped cream or marshmallows, optional

In a medium saucepan over medium heat, combine milk, chocolate chips, and cocoa powder. Cook, whisking, until chocolate chips melt and cocoa powder dissolves. Stir in vanilla extract, peppermint extract, and salt. Remove from heat. Ladle into mugs and top with whipped cream or marshmallows, if desired. Makes 4 servings.

Deck
THE
Home

Perhaps the best
Yuletide decoration is
being wreathed in smiles.

AUTHOR UNKNOWN

Tradition Time

HELEN LOWRIE MARSHALL

So much of the joy of Christmas
Is the sameness of it all—
Always the wreath upon the door,
The festoons in the hall;
The mistletoe hung overhead,
The squeals at getting captured;
The sparkling tree that holds its viewers
Silently enraptured.

The same beloved ornaments,
The candles and the bells;
The same old Christmas stories
That Grandpa always tells.

The same old battered angel
Once again adds to the joy—
It's stood atop the tree each year
Since Grandpa was a boy.

The merry family gatherings—
The old, the very young;
The strangely lovely way they
Harmonize in carols sung.

For Christmas is tradition time—
Traditions that recall
The precious memories down the years,
The sameness of them all.

Christmas at Our House

ELISABETH WEAVER WINSTEAD

White frost on the window,
Green wreath on the door,
The Christmas tree glitters
From ceiling to floor.

Bright candlelight flickers,
The blazing fire glows,
Stockings hang from the mantel,
Lined up in red rows.

The joyous bells of Christmas
Chime through the wintry air,

Greeting happy, smiling people,
Spreading gladness everywhere.

In early Christmas morning,
Our merry carols ring;
It's time for opening presents
And the gifts of love we bring.

As we join in celebration,
May laughter, love, and cheer
Possess each heart on Christmas Day
And through a bright New Year.

Photograph © John Block/Botanica/Jupiter Images

Deck the Home 🎄 51

VISIONS OF A TREE

BEN LOGAN

The search [for a Christmas tree] involved the three children and me, indicating, I think, that Jacqueline had better sense than I did. She waved us on our way and stayed happily behind, the kitchen table covered with mixing bowls, one for each kind of cookie she would make. . . .

Searching for a tree with Suzanne, Roger, and Kristine meant dealing with three fiercely held opinions. It was not just a Christmas tree they wanted. Each had some hidden, inner vision of the perfect icon.

Could they tell me what they had in mind?

No. They would know it when they saw it.

No clues at all?

No. It was impossible to explain it verbally. "It's a feeling-level thing, Daddy."

That would be Suzanne, who had started speaking complicated sentences at ten months and may have been about eight years old when she was born.

Kristine, the youngest, seemed to be looking for something only half-remembered. I would find her staring wistfully at a small, neglected tree that had not won a second glance from the others. I always wondered if it had some connection with the Christmas story about the lonely doll in the store window, appealing in a quiet way that went unappreciated by all who walked by.

Roger, boxed in by age between two sisters, had territory to protect. He had once had an absolute fit when he ran into the truth that, no matter how he grew, Suzanne would always be older. He was less emotionally involved in our search, or at least pretended to be, his demand centering on a more mechanistic vision of the perfect tree. Suzanne, who sometimes has the ability to look over my shoulder even when she is a thousand miles away, would probably say, "Roger just enjoys being oppositional."

> WAS [THE TREE]
> FULL ENOUGH?
> WAS IT BRIGHT GREEN?
> WERE THE NEEDLES
> TOO PRICKLY?

Evergreens in Alpine, Oregon. Photograph © Dennis Frates

Maybe that runs in the family. Suzanne now has an "oppositional" child.

My own questions about the tree were practical. Were the branches stiff enough to support the candles? Did the tree taper enough so that the lower candle flames would not be dangerously close to the next higher whorl of limbs? And, since getting the tree this late means they have all been picked over, could we maybe lower our standards a little?

WE STEPPED BACK AND ADMIRED THE TREE, EACH OF US FINDING SOME DIFFERENT COMPLETION OF A VISION.

No, of course not. And anyway, "You know we never buy one at the first places we look."

Questions. Arguments. Discussion. Did the tree have to be perfect even on the side that would be turned to the wall? Was it full enough? Was it bright green? Were the needles too prickly? Did we like the man or woman who was selling the trees, or did they have "an attitude"?

How does one pursue this mixture of obscure visions and practical demands? Simple. You expose all four people to as many trees as possible, and maybe the perfect one will reach out and say, "Here I am!"

That meant driving all over northern Westchester County, then into Putnam and Duchess counties to all the places selling trees, and then back again to look at trees already seen that were almost perfect, then back to compare those with ones more newly seen, and questions like, "How come we never look for trees in Connecticut?"

"Or maybe New Jersey. Or Rockland County, on the other side of the Hudson River." That was Roger, who was born loving maps, travel, and automobiles.

More discussions and chaos, Kristine wondering more frequently if it was time yet to stop for hot chocolate. Sometimes those were code words for "my feet are cold," something no youngest child ever feels free to admit to older siblings. . . .

I kept track once of our Christmas tree journey. Without ever being more than twenty miles from home, we traveled almost a hundred. On that year, the weather changed. Heavy snow began falling, great flakes coming straight down, quieting the world. That, and other unadmitted cold feet, hastened a compromise. We made our choice and slithered and slid our way home, the tree sticking out the back of the station wagon, getting a coating of wet snow.

The ground was white at home. The dog barked at the tree, wanting to anoint it. We tugged it inside, melting snow decorating the needles with shining beads of water. The smell of pitch joined the smell of just-out-of-the-oven cookies and banana bread, a blend that said Christmas.

Intelligent Jacqueline stayed in the kitchen while new discussion began in the living room. Did the tree have to be in the same place every year? Did we have to cut it off at the bottom, or was it all right for the star to stick up between two beams and touch the ceiling? Was the tree straight, or did I have to put more wooden wedges under one side?

When there was agreement that the tree was straight, of course it had to be turned and become crooked again because another side might look better facing into the room.

I took out the wedges and turned the tree. "Like this?"

"No, I meant turn it the other way."

I turned it the other way and started putting in wedges again.

"Wait. I think it was better the way it was before."

So, out with the wedges. Turn the tree. Put the wedges in.

The tree relaxed in the warmth from the fireplace, the limbs lowering a little. The decorating drops of water dried. We stepped back and admired the tree, each of us finding some different completion of a vision. I looked up, and Jacqueline was standing in the living room doorway, hands clasped together above her apron, looking like a delighted child.

The decorations were already out; Jacqueline sat on the sofa, putting the little wire hangers on ornaments and handing them, one by one, for us to hang on the tree. Like Mamma Grande and like my mother, she held certain ornaments longer in her hands, seeming reluctant to let them go.

The cat appeared, made a wild run into an empty ornament box and slid with it across the floor. She was chased away but came slinking back, batted a low-hanging glass ball from the tree, and pursued it along the wall. She was chased away again. The dog, still sniffing the bottom of the tree in an interested way, was put outside.

The tinseled ropes were draped in spirals around the tree. A bird's nest with an imitation oriole was placed in a whorl of limbs. Then, the candles in their special holders that gripped onto the branches. Last of all, the star at the top . . .

Decorating activity spread through the house. Every window had its figure or bell or snowflake. A string of brass bells was hung on the outside door. A rope for Christmas stockings was strung below the mantel of the living room fireplace.

Snow was falling and darkness came early. I lighted the kerosene lamp with its concave mercury reflector and turned the lamp and tilted the reflector to focus a bright circle of light on the treetop star.

Christmas Wreath

FAIRY WALKER LANE

Decorate a Christmas window,
Holly wreath with berries red;
Bring a thrill of Yuletide pleasure
To the folks who homeward tread.

Light them on their homeward journey,
Renewed with joy throughout the night;
Yours may be the kindly message
That will make their Christmas bright.

The Jolly Holidays

KEN STUDEBAKER

Hail the jolly holidays!
    Alive with joy and cheer:
Holly, snow, and candleglow,
    glad Christmastime is here!

Taste the jolly holidays!
    The Christmas treats abound:
Cookies, cakes, and bellyaches,
    and chocolates by the pound!

Feel the jolly holidays!
    A cold December night:
Frosty lanes and windowpanes,
    a wonderland of white!

Deck the jolly holidays!
    Hang garland, wreath, and spray,
Balsam, pine, the scent divine,
    the smells of Christmas Day!

Ring the jolly holidays!
    A joyous carol choir:

Anthem, song, all sing along,
    lifting spirits higher.

Tell the jolly holidays!
    Stories from the sages:
Angel host and Marley's ghost
    live throughout the ages.

Trim the jolly holidays!
    A sparkling Christmas tree,
Tinsel, lights, the room bedight,
    a joy for all to see.

Bless the jolly holidays!
    The birthday of the King:
Oxen, sheep, the Babe asleep
    while heavenly angels sing.

Welcome, jolly holidays!
    Our favorite time of year:
Parties, mirth, and peace on Earth
    bring joyous Christmas cheer.

Deck the Halls

TRADITIONAL WELSH | TRADITIONAL WELSH

1. Deck the halls with boughs of hol - ly,
2. See the blaz - ing Yule be - fore us,
3. Fast a - way the old year pass - es,

Fa la la la la, la la la la.

'Tis the sea - son to be jol - ly,
Strike the harp and join the cho - rus,
Hail the new, ye lads and lass - es,

Fa la la la la, la la la la.

Don   we now   our   gay   ap - par - rel,

Fol - low me   in   mer - ry meas - ure,

Sing   we joy - ous   all   to - geth - er,

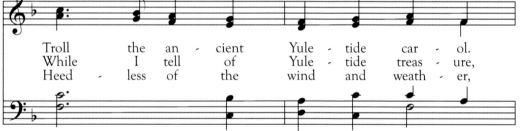

Fa la   la   la   la   la   la   la.

Troll   the an - cient   Yule - tide   car - ol.

While   I tell of   Yule - tide treas - ure,

Heed - less of   the   wind and weath - er,

Fa la la la la   la la la la.

PAPER CHAINS
AND EVERGREENS

JOAN DONALDSON

Hands snug in wool mittens, with stocking caps tugged over their ears, our two sons drag their sleds as we march through several inches of snow. My husband's and my boots swish through the fresh powder that sifted from low-slung clouds that drifted over Lake Michigan during the night. This morning we awoke to the silence of snow-capped pine branches and thousands of glittering crystals. A perfect day for hauling home our Christmas evergreens on sleds. John carries his wooden-handled loppers while the blade of a shovel rests on my shoulder.

We trudge across the pasture while our three goats watch us from their little side door on the barn. Their breath puffs from their noses, and the bells on their collars tinkle as they walk into the paddock for a better view of us. Our boys race each other as we aim for the hedgerows of pine and Douglas fir that border the pasture. We planted these evergreens almost twenty years ago when my husband built our house. That bouquet of seedlings now stands as fifteen-foot-tall trees that stretch from the edge of the field to our pond. Some have dropped pinecones, and now baby pines rise from the needle-covered earth.

> **WE AWOKE TO THE SILENCE OF SNOWCAPPED PINE BRANCHES AND THOUSANDS OF GLITTERING CRYSTALS.**

"Look for a small tree that you would like to dig up," I say. The lads drop the ropes to their sleds and slip through the feathery branches to search for their special Christmas tree.

The fragrance of pine swirls around us as John cuts off low branches and I stack them on a sled. From the firs, I select a pocketful of thimble-size cones. These are our cat's favorite toy, and I know she will bat them beneath the sofa and under the bookcase, stopping only when tempted by a fresh catnip mouse.

"Do you think I've cut enough?" John asks.

"Hmm, just a few more," I reply.

Photograph © Dennis Frates

"How about this tree?" our youngest son calls.

The white pine reaches his shoulders. John sinks his shovel, slicing a wide circle around the tree's base. Finally, the roots loosen and the three of them lift it onto the other sled. We tramp home with both boys pulling the sled with their tree, while John hauls our evergreens. At our front door, he lifts the pine into a waiting pot and settles it into a corner of our great room.

"Let me arrange the lights, and then it's all yours," John says, and the boys open their box of ornaments.

A hand-hewn beam extends across the center of the main room of our timber-framed home. I often wonder what stories the beams of our house could tell us of past Christmas holidays celebrated in settlers' barns. Over the years, John has driven long nails into the overhead beam, and here we array our swags of evergreens.

"You need another one near the west wall," I say and hand John a branch of fir. The branches crisscross along the beam, a wave of pungent needles dotted with fir cones.

Already our advent wreath hangs on white ribbons from the floor joists that support the upstairs loft. Plumes of white pine drape the wooden base. Burgundy rosehips glow beside the puffs of baby's breath, and four beeswax candles rise from the greenery. Tonight when we light three candles, their fragrance will remind me of midnight Christmas Eve services at my grandparents' church and the wonder of walking out of the sanctuary and scanning the heavens for a blazing star.

The boys hang satin balls they've decorated with rickrack and sequins onto their tree and loop a chain of red, blue, and yellow construction paper links. After John arranges the lights across the beam, I lift other ornaments from a tissue-paper filled box. Most are handmade and display the talents and affections of friends. My hands offer John creations given yearly by our friend, Jo, who has cross-stitched small rectangles or folded calico stars. She slipped these gifts into envelopes with her Christmas card, and each one reminds me of her many talents and the days we spent together in college.

John positions a red felt cardinal in the middle of the greenery as our cat swishes her tail, wondering how that bird flew up onto the beam. I search the tissue paper until I find an English walnut wrapped in foil, fashioned by my hands at age three during Sunday school. The memento has endured almost half a century and stirs memories of singing in the youth choir, wearing a white robe with a green bow that tickled my chin. Finally the box is empty, and John positions a translucent globe etched with an angel near a golden light bulb.

"Shall we turn on the lights?" John asks.

The lads plug in the lights on their tree. A spiral of red and blue, green and yellow sparkles around the potted tree, and the satin balls shimmer. Their eyes glow.

Overhead, white stars glitter along the beam, illuminating white angels and their trumpets and the wooden rosettes John crafted on Christmas. The assorted stars and angels, a cut-paper rabbit and clay goat; each ornament is unique, like the friend or family member who created it, and whose love sweetens the season of our lives.

CHRISTMAS ON THE OLD FARM

ANN SILVA

Only a few more days remain before Christmas and the sounds, the tastes, the smells, and the joys that it brings to the farm. Outside, in the frosty, cold farmyard, stands the old smokehouse, weathered a silver gray. Inside the smokehouse are the smells of Grandma's homemade soap, kept in the first room along with hoes, shovels, sickles, and kegs of nails. In the darkened room in the back are hams, sausages, and salted meats in crocks.

Inside the white-frame walls of the farmhouse, hands large and small are busy cleaning and dusting and polishing everything in sight. Silver begins to gleam and sparkle in the gentle light of the fire. Syrup pitchers are full, and the pantry is stocked with apples, pies, cakes, and chocolate fudge loaded with nuts. And there are plenty of Grandma's homemade dill pickles—how we children love them!

THE TREE STANDS IN THE CORNER, TRIMMED WITH GLITTER AND POLISHED APPLES AND ORANGES WRAPPED IN TISSUE PAPER AND TIED WITH RED RIBBONS.

In the parlor, the old pump-organ is opened, decorated for the season with fresh-scented pine and holly boughs. The tree stands in the corner, trimmed with glitter and polished apples and oranges wrapped in tissue paper and tied with red ribbons. The tree will be lit—only on Christmas Eve, and only for a short while—by homemade candles. But we do not need the lights on the tree to tell us it is Christmas. Its aroma, mingled with that of bayberry candles, fills the room; and we know for certain that it is Christmastime on the old family farm.

Photograph © Jessie Walker

Photograph © Jessie Walker

The Red Stocking

CARICE WILLIAMS

This year there's one less stocking
Hung by the fireside;
This year our little girl of eight
Announces with great pride
That Santa Claus no longer
Slips in on Christmas Eve
To fill her bright red stocking,
For she does not believe.

And so when Christmas Eve arrived,
We left the fireplace bare.
But long ere dawn a little girl
Had hung a stocking there.
On Christmas morn her face lit up
At gifts all stuffed inside.
"I still believe in Santa Claus,"
She sheepishly replied.

A Stocking on a Fireplace

PATRICIA ROSE MONGEAU

A stocking on a fireplace
Brings back a memory
Of a stocking on a fireplace
That once belonged to me.

I'd hang it up all by myself
And I'd gaze at it with pride,
Then dream a special dream of all
The things I'd find inside.

And when I woke on Christmas morn,
I'd find to my delight

My stocking filled up to the brim
With treasures gay and bright.

I'd find a doll with eyes that closed,
A ball of shiny red,
Some books, a game, a set of jacks,
A bonnet for my head.

I'd find an apple and an orange,
Some nuts and candy too,
And each year when I found these things,
The thrill was ever new.

THE CHRISTMAS VILLAGE

DANIELLE BROWN

We would remember it the rest of our lives—that one special evening in early December when Dad brought home the colored bristol board and a bag full of wonders.

Anticipation prevented us from keeping still. My siblings and I fidgeted at the dinner table, half sitting, half standing, all eyes shifting from our father to his mysterious supplies.

Through the darkened window, the wind howled, swirling snow around the lampposts. But even the possibility of classes being canceled the next day could not compete with the magic we sensed was about to happen.

At long last, Mom cleared away the dishes and removed the vinyl table-cloth. Dad carefully unrolled the construction paper and spread half the contents of the bag on the table. He checked the blade on the utility knife. Satisfied, he reached for pencil and ruler.

We sat across from him, barely breathing lest we disturb the artist or his tools. At no other time were all five children so quiet and focused. Taking advantage of this respite, Mom tackled her Christmas baking.

Dad drew an elongated cross pattern with different shapes growing out of it. He pulled his head back and studied the geometric design, brows knotted, forehead furrowed. Then he smiled, teasingly glancing at us through his eyelashes, and grabbed the knife. Meticulously following the lines, he cut through the red cardboard.

We watched him, mesmerized, as he folded the bristol this way and that. And there it was, a perfect miniature house!

Red cellophane finished off the two upper windows and the lower front door. Cotton batting became snow on the roof. What other treasures could this bag harbor? Dad fished out tubes of glue and jars of glitters, sending a shiver of

THE SIGHT OF THE CHRISTMAS VILLAGE SET UP ON THE TABLE STOPPED US ON A DIME AND RENDERED US TEMPORARILY SPEECHLESS.

delight through his gasping audience. While he worked on the next house, we armed ourselves with gold and silver dust to make the snow sparkle. We argued over who would get first crack at the house; but in no time, Dad had five little buildings ready. And in no time, there was glue on every flat surface in the room.

The overheated kitchen smelled of cranberries, zesty fruit peels, and chocolate. Mom slid a plate of warm cookies on the table.

Too soon, bedtime came. Dad, exhausted after a long day at work, stretched his arms and rubbed his lower back. It was bedtime for the children, but he would complete the village before retiring for the night. Minus the glitters. We made him promise.

At the crack of dawn the next day, all five of us noisily trooped down to the kitchen. The sight of the Christmas village set up on the table stopped us on a dime and rendered us temporarily speechless.

A blanket of cotton batting covered piles of books of different heights and gave the illusion of snow on hills. Groupings of two, three, and four houses nestled among the peaks and valleys. On the highest knoll sat a magnificent gray church with a tall steeple and a tiny wooden cross.

The normal cacophony resumed as we all spoke at once. Dad halted a fist fight with his decision of putting the sparkles on the church himself. That morning, we ate breakfast standing up. There seemed no point in moving the village as long as work remained to be done.

We were kept busy and in line for the next few days. As completion of the village neared, excitement built up over the trimming of the tree.

By the time our spruce could hold no more icicles, garlands, and pine cones, Mom had baked the last of the Christmas puddings, and we had consumed nearly all the cookies. However, the precious village could now be installed in its permanent home at the base of the tree.

THE ENCHANTING, DIMINUTIVE VILLAGE HAD COME TO LIFE.

Dad duplicated his original work with piles of books and batting, organizing red and green houses in small neighborhoods, placing the church on a plateau. We dusted the batting with glitters, liberally sprinkling ourselves and the dog in the process.

On Dad's instructions, we all went in search of Mom. That must have been when he poked a light through the back of each tiny building. We never saw him do it. I often suspected my mother was in cahoots with him, as I cannot recall a time when the sneaky woman was more difficult to locate. However, having done so, we barreled back to the family room for the lighting of our Christmas tree.

With bulging eyes and mouths wide open, we stared into a fairytale. Under the radiating spruce, the enchanting, diminutive village had come to life. Miniature trees had been planted, old folks strolled down the streets while others sat on park benches. Streetlights glowed softly while every house rejoiced.

Lying on the floor, propped up on elbows, chins firmly cupped in hands, we gawked at the hypnotizing, bright scenes before us. Dad had brought home, in a bag, the world's best Christmas present. And we would remember it for the rest of our lives.

Swirled Peppermint Bark

8 ounces semisweet baking chocolate, chopped

6 ounces white baking chocolate, chopped

½ teaspoon peppermint extract

½ cup peppermint candies, crushed

Divide semisweet chocolate evenly into 2 microwave-safe bowls. Microwave each on high 1 minute; stir until smooth. Microwave an additional 10 to 15 seconds, if needed. Pour semisweet chocolate onto a waxed-paper-lined baking sheet and smooth out chocolate; set aside. Stir peppermint extract into white chocolate. Slowly pour white chocolate over the semisweet chocolate. Swirl chocolates with a knife; sprinkle with crushed candy. Chill until firm, about 1 hour. Lift bark from baking sheet and break into pieces. Store tightly covered at room temperature. Makes about 1 pound of candy.

Candied Tangerine Peel

8 tangerines

2 cups granulated sugar

Superfine sugar

Remove peel from tangerines and cut into ⅛-inch julienne strips. In a medium saucepan, cover strips with cold water; bring to a boil. Drain well and repeat process 2 times. Bring to a boil granulated sugar, strips, and enough water to cover, stirring until sugar has dissolved. Lower heat and simmer until zest is translucent and syrup has thickened, 45 minutes to 1 hour.

Transfer candied peel, separating strips with a fork or tongs, to a large, lightly oiled rack set over a waxed-paper-lined baking sheet. When peel is cool (but not completely dry), toss in superfine sugar to coat. Return to rack until dry to touch, about 1 hour. Store in an airtight container at room temperature up to 2 days. Makes about 3 cups of candied peel.

Chocolate Fudge

12 ounces bittersweet or semisweet chocolate, finely chopped

2 cups toasted walnuts or pecans, chopped, optional

10 tablespoons unsalted butter, softened

1 tablespoon vanilla extract

20 large marshmallows

4 cups granulated sugar

2 5-ounce cans evaporated milk

In a large heatproof bowl, combine the chocolate, nuts (if desired), butter, and vanilla; set aside. In a heavy saucepan over medium heat, combine the marshmallows, sugar, and evaporated milk. Bring to a boil, stirring constantly. Continuing to stir, boil 6 minutes. Remove from heat and immediately pour marshmallow mixture into chocolate mixture; beat constantly until creamy. Quickly pour into a well-greased 9 x 13-inch baking pan, spreading the fudge evenly. Cool at least 1 hour before cutting into pieces; chill if needed to set. Serve at room temperature. Makes about 6 to 8 dozen pieces.

Mom's Divinity

2½ cups granulated sugar

½ cup light corn syrup

2 egg whites

¼ teaspoon salt

2 teaspoons vanilla extract

1 cup coarsely chopped walnuts, optional

12 candied cherries, halved, optional

24 whole pecans, optional

In a 1-quart heavy saucepan, combine sugar and corn syrup with ½ cup water. Over low heat, cook, stirring, until sugar is dissolved. Cover; cook 1 minute or until sugar crystals on side of pan melt. Uncover; bring to boiling, without stirring, to 238°F or until a small amount in cold water forms a soft ball.

Meanwhile, in large bowl of electric mixer, at high speed, beat egg whites with salt until stiff peaks form when beater is slowly raised. In a thin stream, pour half of hot syrup over egg whites, beating constantly at high speed until stiff peaks form when beater is raised. Continue cooking rest of syrup to 256°F or until a small amount in cold water forms a hard ball.

In a thin stream, pour hot syrup into meringue mixture, beating constantly with a wooden spoon. Beat in vanilla; add walnuts, if desired. Continue beating until mixture is stiff enough to hold its shape, about 5 minutes.

Quickly drop teaspoonfuls onto waxed paper. Top with cherries and/or pecans, if desired. Allow to cool and store tightly covered. Makes about 2 dozen pieces.

TREE DRESSING

LESLEY CONGER

We always take our tree down on New Year's Eve; and since we always put it up on Christmas Eve, this makes us the last family in the neighborhood to put a tree up and the first to take it down. We've been battling the children on this score for years, while the tree lights go on in window after window up and down the street. They would have us putting it up earlier and earlier until, I suppose, it would be the first thing we'd do after finally persuading them to throw out the Halloween jack-o'-lantern with the top of his skull hung with long green-and-gray mold and his face caved in with a puckering, toothless, centenarian smile. But we've held out, even against charges of being the meanest parents in town.

Of course, a dry Christmas tree is a fire hazard. But if you take a look at our garage with the car parked in front of it because we can't get it inside, you'll know we aren't really concerned with such a practical reason. The truth is that I can't bear to get up in the morning and start a new year with last year's tree standing there in the living room in a shaft of pale, wintry sun, looking like somebody who just got home from an all-night party—disheveled, exhausted, and footsore. It isn't that we don't like Christmas trees; we just don't want to be tired of ours before we take it down.

So we put the tree up on Christmas Eve. Every other year or so, another child is old enough to join the ritual, another child emancipated and wise with the knowledge that Santa Claus is really Mommy and Daddy and everybody who loves you—and wishing, wistfully, that he weren't, or at least that enlightenment could have been put off just one more year. (But, as childhood's traumatic experiences go, this may not be so much worse than finding out that the plastic model submarine that looks about a foot long on the outside of the cereal package is really the size of the first two joints of your little finger; and it may be that even a six-year-old child can per-

> THE TREE . . . IS ALWAYS A DOUGLAS FIR, . . . ALWAYS AS BIG AS POSSIBLE . . .

ceive, in his heart if not in his head, what lies behind each of the two deceptions.) As for the tree, it is always a Douglas fir, *Pseudotsuga taxifolia*, no exceptions allowed; always as big as possible; and always green. I vaguely recall from years ago a season of aberration, probably adolescent, when I was convinced we ought to have a silver tree with blue ornaments only, but my mother must have prevailed; she could still remember the huge *Weihnachtsbaum* her father and older brothers would drag into the big room of the combination saloon-and-inn the family owned. It was enormous to begin with, but if it were not plump or symmetrical enough to suit them, they would even graft in additional branches to fill it out to perfection. What miserable spindly evergreen sprayed with a silver disguise and hung with ice-cold blue could compete with the memory of such a tree, reaching to the ceiling, smelling of the forest, and quivering with the splendid, dangerous light of candles?

We put our tree up with tremendous seriousness, moving the colored lights from socket to socket and standing back to squint at the effect, worrying about too many reds on one side and too many greens on the other. We hang the balls, lifting each one tenderly from its tissue-paper nest. Some are new, some are older than our oldest child, but there is one neither gold nor silver nor any of the shiny, gaudy colors. It is a satin white with soft green leaves and a velvet peach, and this one I remember from my own childhood; and I hang it myself, trembling each year for fear it might fall and break and my heart with it. Then there are little birds to clip on the branches, and a tiny wooden angel and candy canes and, in years when I am ambitious, decorated

cookies with loops of thread to hang them by, and strings of popcorn and cranberries.

The last thing to go on the tree is the silver rain. I know it says *icicles* on the package, but I have lived most of my life in this immoderately moderate northwest climate, and to me it always looks like rain. We hang the rain patiently, precisely, strand by strand, and anyone who starts to take it heedlessly by the handful and throw it at the tree (a degraded practice followed in some savage quarters) is immediately apprehended with cries of horror and revulsion. But, at last, the sheet is spread beneath the tree; and one of the boys crouches there in readiness, holding the light plug while the rest of us switch off the lamps. A prickly moment of darkness—and we all sigh in unison our skyrocket-bursting, Christmas-tree-lighting-up sigh: "Aaaahhhhh!"

Spirit of Christmas

BERNICE HEISLER

A star-tipped tree
Jeweled with light
Is the spirit of Christmas,
Joyous and bright,
And it brings a wish
Ever warm and sincere:
"Merry Christmas to you
And a happy New Year!"

Christmas Tree

KATHERINE EDELMAN

As we looked backward from the stair
Last night, this corner was quite bare.
Now, we rub our eyes to see,
Beside the wall, a lovely tree
With stars and lights; its fronded green
All laced with strands of silver sheen.
How could a tree so lovely bloom
In one short night in our front room?

THE LAST DAY
OF CHRISTMAS

FAITH ANDREWS BEDFORD

*T*he angel ornament's wing is broken. The penguin is missing one of its skis. The star at the top of the Christmas tree is tarnished and bent.

In the excitement and giddy rush of decorating for the holiday season, little things like these tend to be overlooked. Besides, as my husband points out, if we turn the angel to the wall we can't tell she's a bit lopsided. I always mean to repair the decorations as they go up, but it just doesn't seem to happen.

When it comes time to transform the house for the holidays, I never have to hunt for helpers. Eager hands string the garlands and hang the wreaths. The tree is decorated in the twinkle of an eye. But when January arrives and it's time to take down the tinsel and box up the baubles, everyone disappears.

Taking down our home's holiday finery always left me feeling depressed. Putting away the decorations was once a dreary, lonely job, one that guaranteed a good case of the post-holiday blahs. But not anymore.

*E*AGER HANDS STRING THE GARLANDS AND HANG THE WREATHS. THE TREE IS DECORATED IN THE TWINKLE OF AN EYE.

Several years ago I instituted "the Last Day of Christmas." No longer do I have to pry my husband and son away from the New Year's week football games to take down the garlands. Gone are the days I had to coax our daughters from comfy chairs where they are curled up with their new books to pack up the ornaments. No one has to wheedle our grandchildren away from their brand-new toys. I set some cider to mull on the stove, and the house once again fills with the spicy aromas of cinnamon and nutmeg. We play the Christmas records one last time, merrily singing the carols off-key. Our Christmas decoration box now contains a first-aid kit consisting of such things as a hot-glue gun, thin ribbons, sequins and glitter, snippets of felt, wire ornament hangers, and all sorts of odds and ends that can restore a bedraggled decoration.

In the hurry of decorating the tree, the children often do not stop to

admire each ornament and remember when I gave it to them and why. But as we set up our little clinic and scrupulously examine each ornament for signs of wear and tear, my husband and I reminisce about the little boat that our daughter got when she learned to sail (and whose mainsail needs a bit of mending) or the tiny pickax and coil of rope I gave our son when he climbed Half Dome, in Yosemite National Park. Last year, as I carefully ran a bit of white glue over a crack in a sand dollar I had given my husband, I turned it over and read, "To Bob, Happy Hilton Head Memories, 1980." In an instant I was back on the beach watching our children jump through the waves. We had found many sand dollars washed up on the shore and bleached white by sunlight. With a bit of red ribbon looped through a hole, they made perfect Christmas gifts for aunts and grandparents. I'd saved one for Bob.

This year I look over at our son carefully whittling a popsicle stick to make a new ski for the penguin and remembered the first time he went down a slope all by himself. Drew had been skiing since he was three but always between his dad's knees. Finally when he was six, we put him in a class with three other little boys. The ski school director had shooed us away. "Don't stick around to watch," he urged. "Makes everyone nervous." And so, crossing our fingers, we went off to ski on the other side of the mountain. Drew's instructor's name was Lars; he spoke little English. But when we returned at lunchtime, we stood openmouthed in amazement as we watched him lead his little team down the mountain. "Piece of pie," Lars shouted as the boys immediately assumed a broad-based snowplow position. The little group snaked back and forth across the packed snow and came to a stop in front of us. Drew grinned up at us with pride. Now he is teaching his two little girls to ski.

While our repairs might lack expertise, they sparkle with creativity. The wooden angel's missing wing has been replaced by a feather from an old boa. When the ceramic Santa's hat was broken, someone glued on a thimble. Often the repairs are so outlandish that no one can tell what the original ornament was supposed to be. No matter. A bit of family silliness is just the cure for post-Christmas gloominess. As we dust off the ornaments, we dust off old memories. The Last Day of Christmas has become a chance to extend, just a bit, the merriment of Christmas.

FROM THE

CHRISTMAS

Kitchen

—m—

Christmas is come, hang on the pot,

Let spits turn round and ovens be hot.

Beef, pork, and poultry, now provide

To feast thy neighbors at this tide. . . .

VIRGINIA ALMANAC, 1765

SUGAR SANTA

CATHERINE CALVERT

I know Christmas is about church, and I cherish my moments of caroling while the candle flames shiver in the darkened sanctuary. And I know Christmas is about giving, and I love the hurly-burly of the shops, where I try to fathom what everyone really, really wants, gifts to be wrapped up in silver.

But I know some of the real meaning of Christmastime also lies in the kitchen. The rest of the year I am devoted to olive oil and brown rice. In December, however, I start to buy butter and flour and sugar and Crisco, and move aside those books devoted to Italian country cuisine and French bistro cookery. It's time to dig out the ones I usually neglect: a 1965 Betty Crocker, two pamphlets from church circles in small Southern towns, and a 1944 *Joy of Cooking*. And I fret till I find my prized notebook, with its spattered recipes clipped from old magazines or scribbled after a phone call to my mother—a few even in my grandmother's fine handwriting and Sheaffer's peacock-blue ink. The recipes are a kind of time capsule, documenting who was eating what as the century progressed, and through them I rediscover the reassuring rhythm of the cooking I used to do.

SOME OF THE REAL MEANING OF CHRISTMASTIME ALSO LIES IN THE KITCHEN.

I'm never lonely in a Christmas kitchen. Like as not, I have a daughter at my side, perhaps intent on beater-licking, perhaps something more. We stir and talk. If once humankind huddled around campfires and told tales of the past, I think that now the culture gets handed down in the kitchen, along with the chocolate chips.

"When I was little . . ." begin the tales that I always use to snare Kate and Zara, who are enthralled by the thought that their mother was once young. At Christmas dinner, I tell them for the tenth time, I would wear my best dress with the scratchy petticoat and sit up straight among the aunts and uncles, fiddling with my silverware at a white-draped table, bade to be good beyond bearing. I made my way through the seemingly endless procession of courses, knowing

Photograph © Mark Thomas

what I was really waiting for was dessert—specifically, for my grandmother's sugar cookies, sweet golden moons that accompanied every holiday feast. While my elders munched on their mincemeat pie, I managed to make away with a whole handful. (At our pleading, one of my grandmother's last acts, at ninety-two, was to bake her sugar cookies while we took notes, translating the "pinch" of this and "bit" of that to a recipe card, which Kate now carefully copies into her notebook.)

Then I describe to my girls the disappointing Christmas I had as a teenager, when their grandmother, proud of her new springerle rolling pin, made dozens of those beautiful anise cookies. I avoided them each time they were offered, clearly (and probably unkindly) expressing my preference for the cookies she had always made—the ones you cut out carefully and bake slowly, and on which you unleash your artistic temperament, tinting confectioners'-sugar icing in gaudy hues, outlining angel wings in candy buttons.

When I went to college and got sophisticated, I confess that for a time I disdained such homely creations. I tell my daughters how I brought home a recipe for bourbon balls: so European, I thought. I dug out the dusty bottle of whiskey and baked some, and they rolled, lonely and uneaten, round the cookie plate. Later, alone in New York, in my cute little single-girl's apartment, with a miniscule stove and refrigerator and a kitchen counter that was just three cookie-angel's wings wide, I felt the old stirrings as Christmas approached, and I spent a Saturday with a flurry of flour, till the smell of cinnamon wrapped the halls and floated down the elevator shaft. Monday, I took a boxful off to work, where,

one by one, other newly fledged young women also brought boxes to the office. We sat at our desks, happily trading gingerbread men and butter cookies. . . .

Now, as my daughters and I bake, there is a litany of cookies I focus on, a list that cannot be trifled with, or it simply isn't Christmas. Some are intended for Santa. Some will go out the door to neighbors or teachers, or be munched at odd moments in the weeks before the holiday, part of the anticipation made incarnate in sugar and raisins. But the tins must be full.

My British husband finds our cookie-making unfathomable. For him, Christmas baking means a single endless fruitcake—wrapped in marzipan and royal icing, and eaten in judicious chunks with tea every evening—a ceremony more important than flavor. The girls and I, as ever, are on the side of excess. The cookies that result from one of our baking sessions leave the kitchen looking as if it had snowed confectioners' sugar and rained chocolate, with enough silver dragées in the corners that they're still rolling out in May. For those of us who live well-regulated lives the rest of the year, a cookie bacchanal is a necessity.

Indeed, my girls are well aware that from the moment they were old enough to be propped on a chair next to the counter, a dishtowel tied round the neck, pudgy pink fingers ready to roll a doughball in cinnamon, they were apprenticed to a long tradition. (Even during the depths of the Depression, I remind them, the baking continued in the great-grandmother's kitchen. Date bars and pinwheels, cocoons and snickerdoodles—cookies heavy with butter, sweet with spice, which must have meant some scrimping to afford.)

When Kate and Zara were seven and eleven, respectively, we moved to Germany, far from the chocolate chips of their early childhood. For weeks I scoured the shops for the fixings, then watched our cookies rise and fall and burn in the oven. German flour is different, and after three batches, we sat amid the smoke ruins, gnawing on lebkuchen and dreaming of home.

Just as the girls were climbing, disconsolate, into bed, the doorbell rang, and we opened the door to a hallway empty of anything but shadows and, on the doormat, a plateful of the most beautiful cookies in the world, arranged round a glowing candle. It was St. Nicholas night, and an elderly neighbor, childless and silent whenever we met, had kept the old custom of surprise gifts for children for my daughters. The girls oohed and aahed at each perfect cookie, chocolate glazed, cinnamon-sprinkled, unfamiliar but so welcome.

Now we've added *zimtsternen* to our repertoire, cinnamon stars that remind us of a Christmas when we felt so far from home. Each year, we feel again the power of time spent together cooking—dreaming of the past and catching the moment as it passes, gilded in sugar, spice, and companionship.

Photograph © Jessie Walker

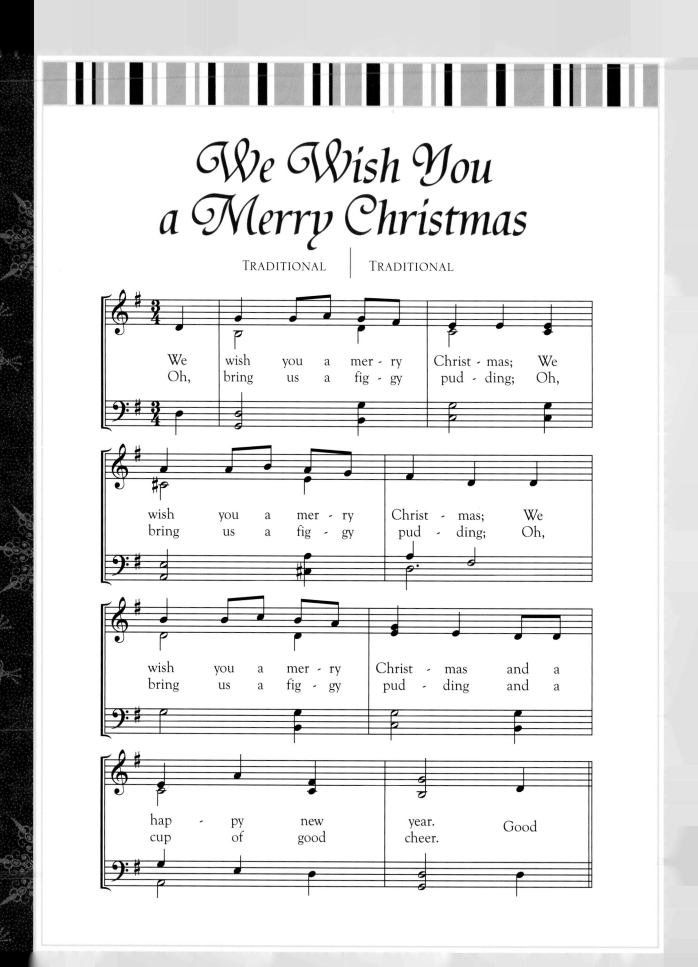

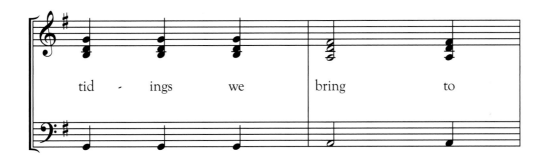

tid - ings   we   bring   to

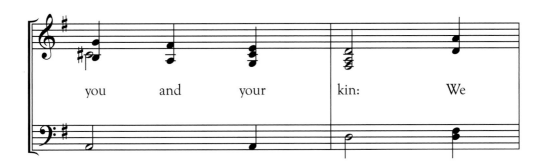

you   and   your   kin: We

wish   you   a   mer - ry   Christ - mas   and   a

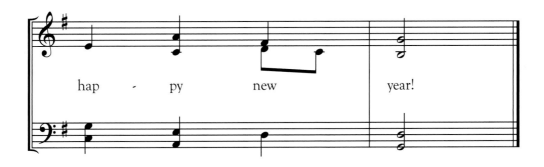

hap - py   new   year!

THE PROOF OF MOTHER'S PUDDINGS

JOY BALE BOONE

As a child, my Christmas began in autumn with the ritual of making Mother's plum pudding. Though the event was temporarily forgotten by me when birthdays, Halloween, and Thanksgiving came along, its sweet solemnity was renewed when the plum pudding, top ablaze each year, made a triumphant entrance into my parents' dining room on December 25.

I was three or four years of age when first allowed to watch the plum pudding ritual. In those days, children started school with kindergarten, not daycare, so it didn't matter which day Mother chose to devote to her one culinary distinction, provided, of course, that it wasn't her weekly day of leisure when friends came to call.

After I entered the primary grades, plum-pudding day always fell on Saturdays. Only when I was older did I realize Mother had accommodated me. When I grew from childhood into my teens, my interests became more outward and lively, and I eventually forsook Mother's day of shared magic. But my guilt is retroactive. I have come to treasure the thought that for nearly a decade, I owned Mother's undivided attention for at least one day each year. I felt honored to stir, bake, and sample in the kitchen with Mother with time out for lunch, for a languorous nap during the early years, and for seemingly endless sips of aromatic afternoon tea.

> AFTER THE FOOD AND FUN CAME THE PUDDING CARRIED INTO THE DINING ROOM. . . .

Other than on those precious plum-pudding days, I seldom saw Mother in our kitchen except when she passed through it to head for the garage, and on to market or to pay a social visit or to pick up a child from school. On Sundays, she would hustle directly from the Episcopal church to give the last-minute touch to the Yorkshire pudding our cook had started. My parents, who came to the States as bride and groom from England, never lost their accents,

their traditions, or their bland Yorkshire puddings. Yet Mother entrusted puddings of the Yorkshire variety to take shape in another's hands. Mother reserved her kitchen presence for the concoction and care of her singular culinary masterpiece: her savory plum pudding.

Mother never encouraged culinary questions. Together in the kitchen, she and I were mostly quiet, speaking—if at all—in whispers. I watched Mother cut pale green citron in ever-smaller pieces. I stood by her side as she carved crystallized orange and lemon peels into sparkling shapes that struck me as a magical, aromatic melding of shapes and colors smooth and glorious as stained glass. And I

As MOTHER PASSED SLICES AROUND THE TABLE, SHE AND I ALWAYS SHARED A SMILE.

can never forget the exotic smells of the mace, nutmeg, and cinnamon Mother blended into the heady mix. Such sights and scents transported me to reveries of Wise Men's myrrh. As Mother labored intently, I saw turbans and casks of gold.

Sound, too, accompanied our solemn plum pudding ritual. Brinky, our brindle bull terrier, snored softly in his basket at the foot of the back stairs. Perhaps he dreamed of sugarplums, those fruits Canadians call saskatoons. Now, as then, it came as a comfort to know that sugarplum trees are more than mere fantasies. The yellow canary in

the adjoining room sang joyously, accompanying Brinky's canine snore, causing Mother's performance to rise to the pinnacle of full orchestration.

After Mother had enriched the pudding's smooth dough with candied fruits, spices, and other delights, she forced the mixture into molds resembling miniature replicas of pyramids I'd seen in full-color, Sunday-school renditions of *The Book of Knowledge*. By then, the water-filled kettles awaited the rich concoction. After Mother steamed the puddings for six hours, she—with help from our maid—cautiously removed them from the stove, while I observed the rite from a respectful distance. Then Mother unwrapped the puddings—usually three or four in number—and gently wrapped them in the flannel cloths I regarded as swaddling clothes. Snug in their warm, brandy-soaked flannel that complemented the sherry with which my otherwise teetotaling mother had sprinkled the dough, the puddings then rested three months or so in the chocolate-colored crocks that lined our pantry shelves.

—⁄⁄⁄—

By early afternoon [on Christmas Day], turkey, stuffing (scooped with our long-handled silver serving spoon), cranberry sauce, a cornucopia of vegetables and salads, and colorful non-food crackers dressed our dining room table. In England, an edible cracker is called a biscuit. A celebratory cracker, a party cracker, is a light cardboard tube covered in colorful paper. When I was young, the covering consisted of red or green crinkly crepe with tinsel of some sort for glitter. A narrow tape with a tiny explosive device at its middle runs through the cracker's tube. We pulled each end of our crackers' tapes so that as they popped and banged, they split apart, divulging favors, fortunes, and paper hats. We partied merrily, we heads with paper crowns!

After the food and fun came the pudding carried into the dining room, flames licking the holly sprig perched high atop the lofty dessert. Not even my father found cause for wit as my mother gravely sliced her pièce de résistance. As Mother passed slices around the table, she and I always shared a smile. The spirits that danced around the pudding's crown as a holiday communion gave way as we drove our sterling spoons into the pudding's dense core, in search of a hidden token. A ring, a charm for a watch chain, a small glass flower, whatever trinket Mother had buried, was meant to hasten good fortune in the lucky recipient's new year. However, I, like my siblings, took heart—we were not the token's finders—in the fact that luck could also be captured and consumed by downing a spoonful of pudding still lit by a flickering flame.

When my mother gentled into advanced age, she spent a few years with my husband, me, and the two children still living at home. She was happy in the presence of books; and though I would frequently find her reading one upside down, I knew she felt content simply from cradling bound pages in her hands. Usually, when she closed a volume at any age, she'd say with satisfaction, "Well, I've finished that one!" Of course, there's more than one way to finish a book.

One quiet evening, as we sat in the library together, I asked Mother if she ever thought about the brandied puddings in their sealed brown crocks in the pantries of our two long-ago homes. For a moment she looked at me very hard. I was afraid I'd offended some delicate balance deep within her. But then her face softened. She smiled. I had my answer. And I hoped her memory proved as fulfilling as mine.

Photograph © Mark Thomas

TENNESSEE CELEBRATIONS

ELAINE YOUNG MCGUIRE

Each year, on Christmas morning, (except for the year my twin sisters had chicken pox), my family followed a routine. We got up early to see what Santa had left. We opened presents and dressed quickly in our brand-new Christmas outfits. Then we headed to Aunt Estelle and Uncle Miles's house in Donelson, a sleepy little town near Nashville.

Our anticipation rose as each mile drew us closer to the Christmas morning family reunion. It was an unforgettable hour-long drive. We turned off the highway, drove past the little schoolhouse, across the railroad tracks, and toward a large stone house—where we turned right—and then straight to my aunt and uncle's new home. This new house was even more welcoming than their old log house had been.

OUR GIFT TO ONE ANOTHER WAS UNCONDITIONAL LOVE.

Though it was Christmas, we never exchanged gifts. Our gift to one another was unconditional love. Excitedly, we ran up to the front steps and straight into the arms of the first aunt, uncle, or cousin to open the door. Love enveloped us.

Our family numbered more than fifty before my grandparents passed on. After that, each branch of the family gathered separately with their own families. But those days would come much later, after I married and moved away.

Back then, my first goal was to seek out my grandparents. Nanny and Dee-Daddy were usually sitting in comfortable chairs near the fire. The mantle was tastefully decorated with fresh evergreens and an assortment of bronze bells from Switzerland, each topped with a red velvet bow. After sharing hugs and kisses, I'd sit down to visit for a while. Satisfied that I'd received a heaping helping of their love, I'd wander off to peek into the big kitchen, where the kitchen help, in their white starched uniforms, would be putting the finishing touches on the meal. Aunt Estelle and Uncle Miles would be right there in the thick of things, making sure everything was done just right. Before they had built their successful dairy business and could afford help, they had prepared the entire dinner themselves. I couldn't fully appreciate their effort until years later when I, like they, had four children of my own to care for.

The kitchen table was an informal gathering spot for those who could hardly wait for eggs to be scrambled and grits to be cooked. The large dining table was reserved for older family members, and card tables were scattered throughout the living room, den, and sunroom to make sure there was room for everyone. All of the tables were covered with starched, white linen cloths and set with fine china, sparkling crystal, and elegant silver. A Christmas centerpiece and candle sat in the middle of each table, making the atmosphere almost magical.

Breakfast would be served at eight-thirty sharp. The call would ring out, "Breakfast is ready!" We gathered around, bowed our heads collectively, and thanked God for His Son, our family, and the bounty set before us. After we had eaten our fill, we wandered off to be with our favorite cousins.

One fateful Christmas Day when I was fifteen years old, my five-year-old brother, Gentry, disappeared with our cousin Stan. They were soon spotted walking on the thin ice of the lake. Our hearts stopped. Once the children understood the danger they were in, we were able to get them to lie on the ice and crawl back to safety. The entire family prayed during and after their rescue. This terrifying event reinforced what we already knew: traditions are important, but faith and family are more important than everything else.

Much has changed since those Christmas days. Times are hectic now, and practicality has replaced formality. Each of the seven branches of Nanny and Dee-daddy's family celebrates the season with its own clan. With a slight twist, my family now shares the traditional Christmas breakfast on Christmas Eve. Aunt Estelle and Uncle Miles' gorgeous house was destroyed by a fire, and Gentry died at the young age of forty-two. Stan and his family continued the dairy business with the same integrity my grandfather and uncle modeled. They have been blessed and now host huge Labor Day family reunions. More than one hundred family members attend, and new cousins get to know one another each year.

Recently, I attended church with my mother and saw Stan's daughter in front of us, bouncing a beautiful baby girl on her shoulder. I smiled at the mother and child and embraced the knowledge that family traditions will continue, despite changing times.

MOTHER'S CHRISTMAS DOMAIN

L. JUNE STEVENSON

*T*he kitchen was Mother's domain. One day in mid-November, the first signs of Christmas preparation would appear. Nuts, fruit, flour, and spices would be on the grocery list. Then, coming into the porch at lunchtime from school, I would spy the plum puddings, wrapped in brown paper and tied with twine, hanging from the ceiling. The house had the warm comfort of sugar and spice. The kitchen table was laden with the ingredients for the dark fruitcake Mother made so well. I got to stir the raisins and peel into the flour before scurrying back to school. Christmas had begun.

> *T*HE HOUSE HAD THE WARM COMFORT OF SUGAR AND SPICE. THE KITCHEN TABLE WAS LADEN WITH THE INGREDIENTS FOR THE DARK FRUITCAKE MOTHER MADE SO WELL.

The cookies were a team effort. I'm sure Mother might have done better without my help. She always let me stir the heavy mixture of sugar and flour, pat out the dough, press my choice of cookie cutter into the dough, and push a piece of red or green cherry into the middle. The first warm shortbread out of the oven was mine. Afterward they were hidden away from grubby fingers in places only Mother knew.

The sugar cookies were next, then the jam thumbprints. I learned to chop walnuts and almonds and to grease the pans. But Mother always grated the nutmeg. Its rich aroma hinted at the coming celebration of the birth of the Christ Child and the arrival of the wise men with gifts of gold, frankincense, and myrrh.

Photograph © Jessie Walker

The Gingerbread Man

GEORGE L. EHRMAN

The gingerbread man was a handsome man,
And he liked Christmas best;
For then my mother always placed
Some jewels on his vest!
Then we would hang him on the tree,
And back and forth he'd sway
And try to be the jolliest
Of all on Christmas Day!

Mom Is Making Christmas

VICKY A. LUONG

Cookies baking in the kitchen—
The smell floats through the air;
Mom is making Christmas
With her usual merry flair.

The house she gaily decorated,
Each gift she stitched with love,
And we'll gather around the Christmas tree
For an evening of old-fashioned fun.

This evening she'll sing a carol for us
With her angel's voice.
Yes, Mom is making Christmas—
A true reason to rejoice.

CHRISTMAS KITCHEN

LILLIAN SMITH

*I*n this cavernous, bright, spice-laden kitchen, the Christmas preparations began late in November, for the fruitcakes were always made early and set aside in the dark pantry to season.

I don't see how my mother could have managed without the big enameled dishpans at such a time. She'd sit at the wide table alongside Big Granny or Little Granny and the cook, cutting orange peel and raisins, citron and ginger and pecans until one of the pans would be filled with the sticky, spicy mess. Then she would measure flour into another pan by the quart and sugar by the pint. She'd leave this, go to the pantry, and come back with a basket filled with six or seven dozen eggs. I liked the creamy-brown ones best and would ask to be permitted to count out the two dozen needed. Then Mother would break them, giving each a sharp nip on the edge of the table and depositing its undisturbed contents, freed of the shell, into the pan. The whole affair was elegant: golden orbs of eggs floating in islands of white . . . Mother's quick, dexterous movements as she went about her work . . . everything calmly moving toward the creation she was intent on. She was an artist in her own kitchen, and there was a deep pleasure in her eyes as she gently pushed prying little ones away and went on with her creating.

> *S*HE WAS AN ARTIST IN HER OWN KITCHEN, AND THERE WAS A DEEP PLEASURE IN HER EYES. . . .

The day came when I must have my try at breaking an egg—which, somewhere in me, had become almost as taboo as setting fire to the house or flinging one of her Haviland china plates to the floor. But now I was seven and grown-up enough to try, and she gave her permission. I stood trembling for five minutes on the edge of that precipice before I could take the fatal step. But I took it; I cracked the egg. Then hesitating again, I brought on disaster by spilling the egg on the floor. But Mother did not scold; she said, "It

happens; let's clean it up." We cleaned it up. Then she said, "Try again." And I tried again and did it. And I am not sure any triumph in my life ever pleased me more than that successful act.

Now, over the fruit and nuts were sprinkled cinnamon and nutmeg and mace and a little grated

ℬUT NO MATTER HOW POKED-OUT I WAS, I MADE A MIRACLE SOMEHOW AND PUSHED IN TWO HELPINGS OF TURKEY DRESSING.

lemon peel. The nuts and fruit and flour and sugar and eggs were finally mixed well together in the biggest pan of all. Someone had greased the four-inch-deep cake pans and lined them with brown paper, and now they were filled and placed in shallow biscuit tins lined with a half-inch of water for the slow steam-baking they required.

But for me, the making of a fruitcake never quite reached the mouth-watering excitement of watching our mother do her famous turkey dressing. To experience this involved your glands, senses, mind, heart, and soul.

It took place on Christmas morning. And no matter how absorbed I might be with new dolls and new books, I'd be on hand to witness this great spectacle.

First, she crushed the contents of a dozen or more boxes of Uneeda Biscuits in a deep bowl. On these crushed crackers she then poured the "essence" which had resulted from browning and

simmering for two hours the neck, liver, gizzard, and wing tips of the twenty-eight-pound turkey. If the essence did not dampen the crackers sufficiently—and it never did—she then "stole," as she said, three or four cups of the most delicious-smelling stock from the turkey roasting pan and added to the mixture. This stealing always sent me into giggles, but I'd keep glancing up at her face to be sure she was joking; for unlike my father she joked rarely, and when she did, she joked so dryly that we were never quite sure she meant it as a joke. Anyway, after the theft of the turkey stock, she put in the dressing six or seven cups of finely chopped celery, a few celery seeds, salt, pepper, a little chipped onion (not much), a half-pound of homemade butter (depending on the richness of the essence), and two dozen eggs. This was well stirred, then two quarts of pecans were added, and two quarts of oysters and a cupful or so of oyster liquor. The whole thing was now stirred for five minutes or more, tasted, a little sage added, a mite more pepper; and then after staring hard at it, Mother would go to the stove, pick up the kettle, and pour a bit of steaming water into the pan to soften it a little more. This was IT. Mother then pushed some of it into the turkey pan—not much, for the turkey was cooking and already had a sausage stuffing in it. Then, after looking at it again for a long moment, and tasting it once more, she poured this delicious mess into deep baking dishes and set it aside to be cooked for thirty or forty minutes shortly before dinner. When served, it would be firm but fluffy, with just enough crispy bits of pecans and succulent oysters.

By this time, the big sisters had filled silver

dishes with candies and nuts and stuffed dates, and glass dishes were filled with homemade pickles and olives; somebody was stuffing the celery with cheese, and someone else was easing the jellied cranberry sauce into one of Mother's fancy flutey porcelain dishes. The cook, or perhaps Big Grandma, had prepared the sweet potatoes for candying; and they were now on the back of the stove, gently simmering in water, sugar, butter, orange peel, and cinnamon. The rice would be cooked during the last twenty minutes before the dinner bell was rung, but already the gravy had been made and thickened with chipped liver, gizzard, and hard-boiled eggs.

The pork salad and Waldorf salad, made early, were kept in the ice-cold pantry until just before dinner when they were placed on the sideboard in two hand-painted bowls. Also on the sideboard were fruit cake, caramel cake, six-layered cake, and several coconut pies. Our father always ate a slice of coconut pie, but the rest of us preferred the traditional ambrosia for Christmas dessert, with a sampling of all of the cakes.

Since the Greeks, there have been ambrosias and ambrosias. Ours was fit for the most exacting Olympian taste, for it was of a special delicacy since the oranges were not sliced but each plug of fruit lifted out of its inner skin and kept as nearly whole as possible. A layer of these fragile orange plugs would be put in the bowl, then a layer of finely grated, fresh coconut (not shredded), then a sprinkling of sugar, then another layer of orange, coconut, and so on until the bowl was full. It might have tasted better served to you as you reclined on a floating cloud, but I doubt it.

And now, the dinner bell rang; and in we ran, already too stuffed by our nibblings since five AM to do more than admire, sniff, and taste here and there. But no matter how poked-out I was, I made a miracle somehow and pushed in two helpings of turkey dressing. The other things could wait until tomorrow or the next day or the next.

All of this was unforgettable, seeping not only into memory but into bones and glands.

Caramel-Walnut Upside-Down Banana Cake

½ cup unsalted butter

1½ cups golden brown sugar, divided

3 tablespoons dark corn syrup

¾ cup walnut halves or pieces

1¾ cups cake flour

1 teaspoon baking powder

¾ teaspoon baking soda

½ teaspoon salt

½ cup unsalted butter, room temperature

½ cup granulated sugar

2 eggs

1 cup mashed, very ripe bananas

3 tablespoons sour cream

1 teaspoon vanilla extract

Whipped cream or vanilla ice cream, optional

In a medium saucepan, bring butter, 1 cup brown sugar, and corn syrup to a boil, stirring constantly until the butter melts. Boil for 1 minute; stir in nuts. Spread topping in greased 9 x 13-inch baking pan; let cool completely.

Preheat oven to 350°F. In a medium bowl, sift together flour, baking powder, baking soda, and salt; set aside. Using an electric mixer, in a large bowl, cream butter, granulated sugar, and ½ cup brown sugar. Beat in eggs 1 at a time; then add bananas, sour cream, and vanilla. Beat in dry ingredients in 2 additions until just combined. Pour batter into prepared cake pan over topping. Bake 50 to 55 minutes. Cool 15 minutes. Invert cake pan onto serving platter. Let stand 5 minutes, then gently lift off pan. Cool 15 minutes or until topping is set. Serve slightly warm or at room temperature with whipped cream or vanilla ice cream, if desired.

Holiday Eggnog Bread

3 cups all-purpose flour

¾ cup granulated sugar

1 teaspoon baking powder

1 teaspoon salt

½ teaspoon nutmeg

1½ cups eggnog

¼ cup butter, melted

1 egg

¾ cup chopped walnuts

¾ cup chopped candied fruits,
  optional

Preheat oven to 350°F. In a medium bowl, sift together flour, sugar, baking powder, salt, and nutmeg; set aside. In a large bowl, beat eggnog, melted butter, and egg. Stir in dry ingredients and mix until just blended. Stir in nuts and fruit, if desired. Transfer to a greased and floured 9-inch loaf pan and bake 60 to 70 minutes. Remove from pan and cool completely before slicing. Makes 1 loaf.

Cherry Cream-Cheese Brownies

1 16-ounce can dark sweet cherries

1 15-ounce box brownie mix

¼ cup vegetable oil

2 eggs, divided

3 ounces cream cheese, softened

2 tablespoons granulated sugar

¾ cup flaked coconut

1 teaspoon almond extract

Preheat oven to 350°F. Drain cherries; reserve ¼ cup cherry juice. In a large bowl, combine brownie mix, oil, 1 egg, and reserved cherry juice. Gently stir in cherries; pour evenly into a greased 8 x 8-inch baking pan. In a medium bowl, beat cream cheese and sugar until well mixed. Add remaining egg and mix well. Stir in coconut and almond extract. Pour cream-cheese mixture into prepared pan over brownie mixture. Use a knife to swirl cream-cheese mixture into brownie mixture. Bake 35 to 45 minutes. Let cool and cut into squares. Makes 16 servings.

CHRISTMAS DINNER

Edna Jaques

My first real memory is of Christmas Day when I was five years old. We used to hang our stockings (two of them held together with a pin) on the back of a chair in the kitchen. Each one had his special chair; mine was near the dining room door. They told us that Santa Claus came down the chimney; as there was a huge coal-burning stove in that room, I figured I'd be the closest one when he landed and would get the most. Why I didn't figure that he would be burnt to a crisp if he came down and into the stove, I don't know; but that is where I hung my stockings.

No GIFT I HAVE EVER RECEIVED IN MY LIFE GAVE ME THE PURE JOY THAT THE LITTLE STOVE DID.

How I wanted a little toy stove! I would ask my mother wistfully if she thought I would get one, and she'd smile her kindly smile and say, "Maybe." Well, I got it. Running down in the dark on Christmas morning, I rushed to my chair; and there it was—a tiny iron stove, about eight inches square, with little pots and pans to go with it, and a tiny teakettle. No gift I have ever received in my life gave me the pure joy that the little stove did. I took it to bed with me for weeks.

We always had Christmas dinner at noon at my grandfather's home, a little house on Cedar Street with two or three lean-tos on it, but cozy and warm with a stove in nearly every room; there was a woodshed at the back with a corner partitioned off for a toilet. How we loved to get out there and see the pictures that Grandma had pasted on the walls: pretty girls, kids, dogs, flowers, plates of apples, and fat ladies in long dresses and floppy hats.

There was a well under the house with a pump in the kitchen, a huge iron thing that fascinated us. We used to make a beeline for it the minute we got into the house and start to pump. But if they saw or heard us coming, they tied the handle to the main pipe; how disappointed we would be if the pump was "tied."

At Christmas, my grandmother would have a long table set in the dining room, which was two steps up from the kitchen. There was a bedroom at one end with the fattest, biggest feather tick I ever saw in my life. On it was a white spread. A little bureau and washstand stood in one corner, and there were a couple of braided rugs on the floor.

At the other end of the dining room was a door that led into a tiny parlor where we hardly dared to go. We would tiptoe in, half-scared, as it was never opened except on Christmas Day. It had a queer musty smell that scared us to death, and we never stayed long in there, I can tell you.

There was a big bay window in the dining room where Grandma kept her flowers. I loved it, with the bright red geraniums and shamrocks and foliage plants with lovely leaves. All my life, I have kept in my heart a picture of that window and wished I had one, but I never got it.

For me, the big event of Christmas Day was the moment where Grandma would come into the kitchen from the woodshed (where she had an extra cookstove). There was a little step, and up she'd come carrying a huge platter with a golden-brown turkey on it. Her face would be red as fire, but there was a sort of triumphant look on it, as if, for her too, this was the crowning event of the year.

There was always a good crowd of us: Dad's brother, John, and his wife and three lovely daughters; Aunt Hattie and Uncle Gilford Pearsall; Byron, the youngest son; and our seven, which included the two big brothers, myself, and two little sisters.

Granddad would say grace, then the carving and passing dishes and laughter would start, everyone praising Grandma's cooking and enjoying pick-

les, jelly, beets, cranberry sauce, homemade catsup, and mashed potatoes, with brown gravy dripping across the plates. For dessert, we ate mince pie and plum pudding until we were stuffed to the gills and hardly able to walk away from the table.

The afternoon was spent with everyone talking and getting ready for supper, which would consist of cold turkey, rich home-canned fruit, Christmas cake, and cookies.

About nine, Maw would gather her little family up, wrap us in our warm coats and bonnets and scarves. Dad would carry the baby home, and all of us would walk in the middle of the road, loving the snow under our feet and the shine of the full moon; finally, there would be the lovely opening of the door and settling into our warm beds.

Photograph © Jessie Walker

104 🎄 HOME FOR CHRISTMAS

Photograph © Jessie Walker

Christmas Dinner

ALICE KENNELLY ROBERTS

The heart remembers Christmas
And days of long ago
When festive preparations
Made all the house aglow;
The kitchen fairly bubbled
With turkey, puddings, pies,
And all those extra goodies
Which came as a surprise.

Each person had his duties,
And old and young could share.
The little ones and Grandma
And even "Sport" were there.
The fruitcake and the mincemeat,
The chestnut dressing too,
The pumpkins and red apples
Filled childhood's world anew.

Yes, hearts go home at Christmas
To take again their place,
To see at Christmas dinner
Each dear, remembered face;
And though the scene we cherish
A short while will be there,
The words, the joy, the laughter
Are with us everywhere!

THE CHRISTMAS EVE
FEAST CONTINUES

Rita Woodhull

*P*reparations for my family's Christmas Eve feast began on December 23, when Mother started baking the holiday bread.

We lived in Connecticut, and the temperature during this snowy time of year hovered around the freezing point. My two brothers, two sisters, and I were usually outside playing; and as the daylight faded, we would come bursting into the kitchen, where we'd be greeted by the aroma of freshly baked bread, mingled with the scent of oranges and anise. As we took off our jackets, mittens, and hats, we began to warm up in anticipation of what was to come. We always sampled the Christmas bread as soon as it came out of the oven.

It was a pleasure to watch my mother cut through the hot, golden crust, then quickly spread each slice with butter that immediately melted. Sometimes we spread olive oil on the warm slabs and sprinkled each with oregano—a treat learned from our Italian ancestors. The untouched loaves would be placed in a large wicker basket, lined and covered with a white tablecloth—ready for our Christmas dinner.

*W*E ALWAYS SAMPLED THE CHRISTMAS BREAD AS SOON AS IT CAME OUT OF THE OVEN

The next morning, Mother would rise early to begin preparing the holiday meal. Getting up early was not one of her favorite things. But on this day, she was happy to be the first one up. She poured some hot coffee and added cream from the top of a milk bottle.

The scallops and fresh fillets were washed, breaded, and refrigerated until they could be cooked. Then the shrimp were boiled with garlic, lemon, and spices before they were peeled and deveined, to be served later in the Mediterranean meatless stew.

All day long, Mother would sing Christmas carols and other popular tunes of the season, accompanied by the kitchen radio. When the radio was off, she'd sing along with fast-moving Italian folk songs on our phonograph.

In the years since Mother passed away, I've tried to prepare the meal just as she did to preserve family tradition. I'll never forget one year when the whole family pitched in.

Our son and daughter and their families were with us. And our youngest son came home from college to celebrate the season with our youngest daughter, then a sixth grader.

I was recovering from a bout with pneumonia and went to bed early. I hadn't baked the Christmas bread, but I planned to get up early to do that and prepare the rest of the traditional feast. When the sun rose, so did I. I dressed and hurried downstairs, but before I reached the bottom step, I was met by the heavenly aroma of freshly baked bread, mingled with oranges and anise. It smelled exactly like our home in Connecticut when I was growing up!

A fire was burning in the fireplace, orange rinds smoldering in the burning embers. When I lifted the white tablecloth covering the wicker baskets on the kitchen table, I found two beautiful loaves of golden bread, their crusts lightly sprinkled with aniseed.

As the warmth of the moment flowed through me, I plugged in the coffeemaker and took some cream from the refrigerator. Then I turned on the radio and got ready to continue the tradition.

Photograph © Elizabeth Whiting & Associates

The Importance of Traditions

EDITH SCHAEFFER

Our traditions connected with Christmas are very special. Our four children and their families have their own careful Christmas traditions—some are the same ones we had and some are different ones. For all of our twenty-eight years in Switzerland, we have had the five o'clock Christmas Eve service in Champéry, with over a hundred candles to be put in wooden candleholders made of rough logs and also fastened on fresh green trees. The supper at home has always started with cream of tomato soup with salted whipped cream on top, and has had a main course of easy-to-serve ham and potato chips and salad with special trimmings and homemade rolls. The apple-mince pies with crisscross crusts (or pumpkin if you would rather) are also a traditional dessert. The Christmas tree has been trimmed the night before, during a traditional time of drinking iced ginger ale and eating homemade Christmas cookies spread out in lovely rows on a tray. The Christmas stockings, filled with all sorts of interesting but inexpensive things, are the old hand-knitted stockings our girls wore the first years in Switzerland. Full of holes, but still usable, they add much in the way of memories as they are pulled out one night and filled and then found on Christmas morning. There are always tangerines to be eaten as we come to them, and homemade Christmas bread, along with tea or hot vanilla eggnog, to be enjoyed in the bedroom as we open the stockings. The traditional lunch of homemade rolls (filled with thin beef), tomato juice, olives and pickles, and either milk shakes or ginger-ale floats for dessert is eaten whenever we feel hungry, sitting around the Christmas tree, opening gifts. There is the customary reading of Luke 2 and prayer together before eating. For dinner in the evening, there is a traditional tablecloth of lovely thin linen with appliquéd deer on it (bought at a sale in Philadelphia twenty years ago and used every Christmas since).

There is something about saying, "We always do this," which helps to keep the years together.

> THERE IS SOMETHING ABOUT SAYING, "WE ALWAYS DO THIS."

Home

AROUND

THE

Tree

The best of all gifts around any
Christmas tree: the presence of a happy
family all wrapped up in each other.

BURTON HILLIS

THE STARS ARE BRIGHTLY SHINING

PATRICIA PENTON LEIMBACH

A poetic fire flickers on the hearth, a couple of fragrant candles glow, and a red poinsettia lends a glory to the room. Paul and the boys have stretched and yawned, looked to the morrow, and gone to bed. I sit alone in the lamplight, as in many a Christmas week of yore, working some gift of embroidery.

A piece of needlework is as much a work of fantasy as it is of art or craftsmanship. But take this vacant chair, put your feet on the hassock here with mine, and I'll share some of the musing sewn into this linen along with the blue floss. It is to appearances a tiny church flanked by evergreens in relief against a night sky. The clock on the church tower says midnight. The sky is studded with stars . . . stars in the mind's eye of the embroideress. In her reverie, this is a tapestry woven with the bright and varied threads of Christmases past.

THIS IS A TAPESTRY WOVEN WITH THE BRIGHT AND VARIED THREADS OF CHRISTMASES PAST.

There she is at five or six, already excited at the shape of a doll box. This one reveals a baby doll with a cloth body and pink plaster head, hands, and feet. Later there would be dolls of rubber, dolls that opened and closed their eyes and cried and wet their diapers, dolls with painted hearts, and stiffly beautiful Shirley Temple dolls with frilly dresses and shiny hair, pretty to look at, disappointing to hold.

There's our Christmas tree in '47—nearly perfect. Brother Bill "made" it himself. It was the last one Frankie Linn had on the lot, tall and spindly with great spaces between branches. The price was right, so Bill dragged it home, sawed it apart, and spliced it together with lengths of pipe. So splendid! Decorated with those snow-covered cottages, lights shining through tiny cellophane windows, and that peculiar star Mary bought during the war with her hard-earned money.

She held three jobs at once as a college student and still found time to make

nearly all her Christmas gifts. One year, there was a woolen scarf threaded with yarn fringe; another year, an orange pomander ball that left a permanent scent of spice in the china cabinet. . . .

Here we are in the kitchen, Mama and I, when I was older and trying to master the old family cooking secrets, making plum pudding, cutting suet into tiny pieces, working in the figs and dates with our hands. Such awful stuff to emerge from the steamer tasting so good as the climax of the feast— dark and rich and fruity, served on the glass plates with lemon sauce.

And my older brothers here, coming in sheepishly on Christmas Eve with great boxes of lacy things, asking, "Do you suppose you could wrap this for Alice? . . . for Mabel? . . . for Gerri?"

Woven into this corner, the Christmas dance of my college dreams—my junior year, at the Hotel Cleveland with my Prince Charming of that year. Just smashing I was, in my green velvet strapless, the sewing project of one entire December, and the African kidskin coat brother John had lavished

upon me. John was there too with my little college roommate. We drank our first champagne that night from a silver loving cup. Oh my! Christmas itself was an anticlimax.

Here's the honeymoon Christmas in Florida, a red flannel nightgown for a gift, both of us a little blue spending our first Christmas away from home, but not admitting it. And from then on there were little boys at Christmas—one, then two, then three—and drums and trains, sleds and ice skates, tractors and popguns. Little boys lighting Advent candles, being angels and wise men, struggling with Scripture, trying to make sense of the Christmas story. . . .

So many years of sewing and wrapping all night, crawling into bed at gray dawn as the boys awoke. So many years in the lamplight of midnight, sewing. . . .

Above the little church I outline one final star, bigger and brighter than the others, the eternal Star of Bethlehem—the star on the tree, the star in the eyes, the glow in the heart, the Hope of the world— golden threads in a Christmas tapestry.

Photograph © Diane Diederich/iStockphoto

Christmas Secrets

AILEEN FISHER

Secrets long and secrets wide,
brightly wrapped and tightly tied;
Secrets fat and secrets thin,
boxed and sealed and hidden in;
Some that rattle, some that squeak,
some that caution "Do Not Peek."

Hurry, Christmas, get here first,
get here fast . . . before we burst.

The Waiting Game

JOHN MOLE

Nuts and marbles in the toe, an orange in the heel,
A Christmas stocking in the dark is wonderful to feel.

Shadowy, bulging length of leg that crackles when you clutch,
A Christmas stocking in the dark is marvelous to touch.

You lie back on your pillow, but that shape's still hanging there.
A Christmas stocking in the dark is very hard to bear.

So try to get your sleep again and chase the hours away.
A Christmas stocking in the dark must wait for Christmas Day.

WRAPPING UP
A MEMORY

CATHERINE CALVERT

Christmas 1957, and all was steeped in darkness. But then, that's natural, since it was only half-past five in the morning. The children, who had lain awake whispering bed to bed, listening to the clock tick till the unheard-of hour of eleven, had been up for an hour, little engines of excitement, ears cocked for the faintest sound of stirring in the parents' bedroom.

I, the oldest, stretched my legs in my pajamas-with-feet and hatched a plot with my sister. We padded down the hallway, our plastic soles going *whisper-whisper*, and crept into our little brother's room, where he lay in his crib, a yellow-haired, pink-cheeked heap. It only took a little pinch before he was bolt upright and screaming for Mother, and the lights flipped on; and we scurried to the door of the living room. "Can we go in now? Can we go in now? Everybody's up. Can we go in?"

THE CHILDREN . . . HAD BEEN UP FOR AN HOUR, LITTLE ENGINES OF EXCITEMENT. . . .

We were, like all children, flexible moralists. We weren't allowed in the room with the tree, and we weren't to wake our parents. We honored the first prohibition and played havoc with the last. For who, impaled on anticipation like a medieval martyr, could stay in bed till the sun rose?

We had been good. We had patiently performed every step of December's rituals: sung in the pageant, worn scratchy petticoats to the officers'-club party, and watched the candle gutter in our hands as we left the Christmas Eve service. But now we were down to the very heart of Christmas.

Presents.

In the days when home movies required the lighting of a Hollywood set, we had to stay frozen in place until the lighting system was operating. It made the living room a magic place with shadowy edges and floodlit center that caused our sleepy eyes to squint as we began burrowing in the present heap. Some families arrange their gifts in piles, some choose an official distributor, and the Queen of

Photograph © Steven Randazzo/SuperStock

England has the servants set up tasteful little tables of presents for each member of the family. We, however, tore into the mound and ferreted out our own until our pile tottered.

There was the unwrapped Big Present, perhaps a bike shining behind the tree branches. There were all those aunt-and-uncle presents—promising, but you can never tell with aunts and uncles. And grandparent presents, though we had one set who were mitten-givers, and consequently not to be looked to for real excitement. And there

WHAT WE WANTED OF GIFTS . . . WAS A DOSE OF DELIGHT, AND EVEN MORE.

were those from Santa Claus, who visited well into our teens, a man of uncanny sense and nonsense.

If all was a flurry till we were settled, Mother on the sofa with the writing pad for thank-you-note reminders, Father fiddling with the framing of the shots (and managing to get endless pictures of children just as they turned their backs to the camera), we were nearly silent as we approached the gifts, selecting each one to be opened slowly, with concentration. There were the practical presents to be held up to the camera, and—if the predictable hat or scarf—to be donned and modeled. There were the intuitive presents from those who knew us—just the book series I was reading, just the kind of toy ponies I was collecting. And then the heart-stopping gifts of imagination that those who loved us managed to produce, such as a dollhouse complete down to the fireplace implements,

with handmade curtains and a tiny sewing machine with a real treadle.

And, of course, there were the gifts that weren't there, the secret longing unsatisfied, as much a part of the morning as the sharp shatter of candy cane in the mouth. For we did, and do, expect a lot out of our presents. As early as October, we'd begun to haunt the toy department, with its intoxicating smell of new dolls, and the beginnings of Barbie's lifestyle on parade. We'd pored over the Sears catalog, counting up the items that came in one doll's trousseau over another's. Then the delicious terror of putting together a list. Ask for one big thing? Spread the goodwill into several lesser ones? (And there were secret desires kept close, like that amazing ballerina doll whose feet could really swivel en pointe. "I'll see if there really is a Santa Claus. He'll know.")

For what we wanted of gifts, then and now, was a dose of delight, and even more: something that expressed recognition of ourselves. Quite a freight for a box. It could go very wrong. I remember the gruesome Christmas when I, known to be bookish, received from well-meaning relatives three copies of *Winnie the Pooh* in Latin and a shirt embroidered with a bespectacled owl, while my little blonde sister squealed as she unwrapped a white fluffy kitten and a bottle of bubble bath. Or the times on the cusp of adolescence when I didn't know quite what I was, and turned my nose up at new ski jackets, secretly longing for one more doll.

You know you've grown up when you remember what you've given for Christmas, rather than what you've gotten. Perhaps one of the burdens of adulthood is losing the sense that all dreams can be contained in a tantalizing square box, gaudy with wrapping paper. For those of us nurtured on Christmases that were bacchanals of present-mongering, sitting down in one's robe to a discreet pile of gifts, nice as they may be, bought by a loving husband who had asked for a list of wants and patiently filled it, leaves me with a tiny, childish wisp of regret. Where, says that nasty little voice in the back of my head, is the ballerina doll? Where's my surprise?

But then, we come from different traditions, my Scottish husband and I. My first visit to Scotland with him was at Christmastime, and I'd jettisoned outfits from my suitcase to make room for the splendors I'd carefully chosen for each member of his family, as yet unknown to me. As I put my bundles under their tree, I felt my usual Christmas Eve bubble of excitement, sure they'd love my gifts.

Up early, I waited through the day—through the oatmeal, the church, the Christmas lunch, the port and cigars, the brisk walk with the Labrador, the steaming teakettle and Christmas cake—before I drew Alasdair aside and hissed, "The presents, what about the presents?" And he, bemused, summoned the family, who looked at my brightly wrapped boxes and opened them carefully, thanked me, then exchanged woolen socks with one another and poured more champagne. And I knew the culture gap was wider than it seemed.

The solution, of course, was to have children, on whom I could work my Christmas magic. "Don't they have enough?" asks Alasdair. "What's 'enough' mean?" say I, and start next year's Christmas shopping at the January sales, and listen hard all year for the "I wants" that aren't fad-

driven. I'm thrifty and foresighted, but I still end the week before Christmas in the stores, searching for just the right dream-in-a-box, threading my way through the crowds, the bustle as much a part of my holiday joys as trimming the tree.

And if, down the hall, the children toss and turn on Christmas Eve, I'm almost equally excited. Did I guess right? Was this really the year Zara would like that book I picked out, and will Kate's love of kittens find reflection in this gray stuffed marvel that meows? And, the next morning, I take my place on the sofa with the thank-you-note list. I watch their eyes kindle and their breath catch as Kate snuggles her kitten, unwilling to lift a hand to open another box, and her sister sits amid the wrapping paper, turning the pages of her book, and my husband fiddles with the camera, wrapping up a memory.

Photograph © Jessie Walker

My House Is Clean for Christmas

MARY E. RATHFON

My house is clean for Christmas now,
That is, except one nook,
Where, through a solemn vow I made
I promised not to look.

I heard my little girl slip in
From school the other day
And softly climb the creaky stairs
To hide a gift away

That she had made all by herself
For no one else but me,

And then beneath the bureau placed . . .
Sure of security.

So, when she heard me say I'd clean,
She made me promise not
To move the bureau in her room,
But clean around the spot.

So, though my house is Christmas cleaned,
One place is filled with dust.
But what's a little thing like that
Compared to my child's trust?

For the Children or the Grownups?

AUTHOR UNKNOWN

'Tis the week before Christmas and every night
As soon as the children are snuggled up tight
And have sleepily murmured their wishes
     and prayers,
Such fun as goes on in the parlor downstairs!
For Father, big brother, and Grandfather too,
Start in with great vigor their youth to renew.
The grownups are having great fun—
     all is well;
The children don't know it, and Santa
     won't tell.

They try to solve puzzles, and each one enjoys
The magical thrill of mechanical toys;
Even Mother must play with a doll that
     can talk,
And if you assist it, it's able to walk.
It's really no matter if paint may be scratched,
Or a cogwheel, a nut, or a bolt gets detached;
The grownups are having great fun—
     all is well;
The children don't know it, and Santa
     won't tell.

Cinnamon Rolls

2 0.25-ounce packages active dry yeast	Cooking spray
¾ cup warm water	8 tablespoons butter, softened
¾ cup vegetable shortening	Cinnamon
½ cup granulated sugar	1 to 1½ cups packed brown sugar
2 teaspoons salt	Raisins (optional)
¾ cup boiling water	Pecans, chopped (optional)
2 eggs	1 16-ounce box confectioners' sugar
4 to 4½ cups bread flour	⅓ cup milk
	1 teaspoon vanilla extract

Dissolve yeast in warm water; let stand until foamy, about 7 minutes. In a large bowl, cream together vegetable shortening, sugar, and salt. Add boiling water; mixture will melt. Quickly beat in eggs. Add yeast mixture and flour; mix until sticky dough forms. Cover and let rise 1 hour.

Spray two 9 x 13-inch baking dishes with cooking spray; set aside. On a lightly floured board, roll out dough into a 12 x 24-inch rectangle, ⅓- to ½-inch thick. Spread with softened butter and sprinkle generously with cinnamon. Top with a layer of brown sugar, raisins, and pecans, if desired. Move the dough so the 24-inch side is in front of you; roll tightly away from you, so dough forms a long jellyroll. Slice into pieces about ¾-inch thick. Place rolls into prepared pans; rolls should be touching. Cover and let rise in a warm place 1 hour.

Preheat oven to 375°F. Bake rolls for about 20 minutes or until golden brown. In a large bowl, whisk together confectioners' sugar, milk, and vanilla until smooth. Spread immediately over hot rolls. Serve warm.

Mama's Porridge

3 cups water
1 cup powdered milk
1½ cups rolled oats
½ teaspoon ground cinnamon
½ cup raisins

½ teaspoon vanilla extract
3 eggs
4 teaspoons butter, divided
1 cup milk, divided
Honey

In a large saucepan, bring the water to a boil. In a medium bowl, combine powdered milk, oats, and cinnamon; quickly stir into the boiling water. Return mixture to a boil, then reduce the heat and simmer 5 to 10 minutes or until the mixture is the desired thickness. Remove from heat and mix in raisins and vanilla. Beat in the eggs 1 at a time, mixing well after each. The hot porridge will cook the eggs completely. Divide the porridge between 4 bowls. Top each with a teaspoon of butter, ¼ cup milk, and a drizzle of honey. Makes 4 servings.

Christmas Breakfast Casserole

1 pound breakfast sausage, spicy or mild
1 large onion, chopped
½ cup diced green bell pepper
½ cup diced red bell pepper
6 slices loaf bread, cubed

6 eggs
1½ cups lowfat milk
1 cup shredded Cheddar cheese
Salt and black pepper

In a large nonstick skillet, crumble sausage and begin to brown over medium-high heat, stirring occasionally. Add onions and peppers to the sausage. Cook until sausage is browned. Drain grease and set aside.

Place bread cubes into a greased 11 x 7 x 2-inch baking dish. Sprinkle sausage mixture over bread. In a small bowl, whisk together eggs and milk. Pour over sausage, pressing mixture down until bread is moist. Sprinkle cheese on top. Add salt and pepper to taste. Cover and refrigerate overnight.

Preheat oven to 375°F. Bake, uncovered, 40 to 45 minutes or until browned and puffy. Cool 10 minutes; cut into squares to serve. Makes 6 to 8 servings.

THE CUT-GLASS CHRISTMAS

SUSAN ALLEN TOTH

The December after my father died, when I was seven and my sister nine, we worried about Mother. We knew she was going to feel bad on Christmas Day, and we wanted to do something special, but we didn't know what. We huddled in the bathroom, whispered in corners, argued intensely in our bedroom after lights out, and, unusually for us, we finally agreed. We would be Mother's Santa; we would fill a stocking for her this year, just as she did for us. How surprised she'd be Christmas morning to see her very own stocking hanging there on the drawer pulls of the maple bureau in our living room. We were sure that would cheer her up.

A week before Christmas, we emptied our piggy banks and set out for Woolworth's, where we always bought our presents. Woolworth's was the Santa-Claus-and-Christmas-tree part of Christmas. It blazed with lights in the after-school dark, smelled of peanuts and popcorn at a counter piled high with chocolate-covered cherries and cellophane-wrapped red-and-white candy canes, rang with "Jingle Bells" and "Hark the Herald Angels Sing" on a radio tuned up loud near the cash register. It sparkled with rows of brilliant glass balls, tinsel ropes, and lights that bubbled when you plugged them in.

First we headed for our two traditional counters for Mother's presents, cosmetics and kitchen utensils. Although Mother never wore makeup, I wouldn't give up hope, encouraging her with a fake tortoiseshell compact of red rouge, or a tiny bottle of Evening in Paris perfume, or a set of mascara brushes. My sister was fond of small silver funnels, metal straining spoons, glass measuring cups. But this Christmas we felt none of our usual gifts would be quite right for a special stocking. We wandered up and down the rows, pondering pencil sharpeners, packaged stationery in floral cardboard boxes, embossed leather billfolds. We rejected a card of assorted needles

> WE WOULD BE MOTHER'S SANTA; WE WOULD FILL A STOCKING FOR HER THIS YEAR, JUST AS SHE DID FOR US.

from England, a fat red pincushion with an attached strawberry-shaped emery ball, an earring tree. The tree was gold-colored metal and spun on a plastic base, but Mother didn't wear earrings.

At last we found ourselves together, discouraged, at a back counter, hidden behind toys and semidarkened under a burned-out fluorescent light, where Woolworth's kept its glasses, dishes, pots, and pans. We knew we couldn't afford a teakettle or frying pan. Mother used empty jars for glasses, and she didn't need any more silverware. But suddenly we both saw at the far end of

the counter a section of cut-glass dishes, not just plain round cereal bowls, but jagged and deeply carved dark green glass. Small bowls were ten cents, a size big enough for soup or oatmeal was twenty. I picked up one and hurried to the end of the counter where it was brighter. How the glass shone! My sister agreed that the fancy dishes were unlike anything Mother had. With our allowances pooled, we could buy six small bowls and two big ones. The clerk at the front packed the dishes carefully in newspaper and warned us to unpack them gently. The edges were sharp, she said. We hurried home in the dark, happy and warm inside with our secret. Eight cut-glass bowls! Mother would never have had such a Christmas.

On Christmas Eve my sister and I faced our only other problem: what to use for Mother's stocking. We both had red-felt Christmas stockings, hung year after year, but we hadn't enough money to buy one for Mother. While Mother was washing dishes after supper, we tiptoed down the hall into her room and began to rummage through her dresser. Winters were cold in Iowa, and Mother had several pairs of sensible cotton and wool anklets, but none of them seemed big enough. We could barely fit one small bowl into each sock. My sister lifted out a cardboard packet. "What about these?" she said. We looked at each other, then at the beige silky stockings, never worn, folded neatly around the cardboard. Mother didn't have many nylons; this was just a few years after the war, and they were still expensive. But we knew these stockings would be big enough to hold our dishes. "I think if we're careful, it'll be okay," I said. We hurried out of the bedroom with the nylons hidden under my sister's skirt.

Early Christmas morning we crept out of our

beds, barely breathing as we passed Mother's door, desperately hoping she wouldn't hear our feet on the creaky wooden stairs. In the living room we hurriedly stuffed her stockings, using both nylons, yanking them wide to accommodate the jagged edges of the cut-glass bowls. We didn't try to hang them up. They were too heavy. Instead we propped them against the bureau that we used for Santa in the absence of a fireplace. Then we looked at bulging stockings, grinned with pleasure at each other, and ran to the staircase to call Mother.

When Mother sleepily entered the living room, her eyes immediately riveted to the bureau. Two green cut-glass bowls hung precariously over the tops of her stretched, snagged, new nylon

*E*IGHT CUT-GLASS BOWLS! MOTHER WOULD NEVER HAVE HAD SUCH A CHRISTMAS.

stockings. "My," she said. "Did you girls do all this?" There was something odd in her tone, but she quickly recovered. "What absolutely beautiful bowls," she said admiringly, sitting down on the floor and taking them out, one by one, setting them in a row on the floor for us all to enjoy. She hugged us both. We were so proud we had pleased her. "You are wonderful girls to have thought of this, and I love you both very much," she said. She ignored the empty stockings sagging on the floor beside her.

Now a mother myself, living alone with an eight-year-old daughter, at Christmas I think of many things, but I always remember that Christmas of the cut-glass bowls. To me it shines as a beacon

my mother left me, a beacon to guide me through the maze of conflicting feelings, emotional demands, free-floating guilt and worry that afflict me at Christmas. When my mother looked at those ruined stockings and ugly cut-glass bowls, which eventually disappeared into the deep recesses of her bottom shelves, she knew what Christmas was all about: "I love you both very much."

It is often hard for me to remember what Christmas is all about. As a teacher on the semester plan, I always find myself buried under term papers and final examinations just before Christmas, a weight that may not be lifted until New Year's, when grades are irrevocably due. Meanwhile a mountain of mail begins to build up on my dining room table, aunts, cousins, dear old friends, all of whom need to hear from me. I have presents to wrap, hurriedly, at the last minute. My daughter has sudden desperate desires to make things; the tree needs to be planted firmly in its stand, lighted, decorated; where are the candles that always go on the mantel? Marking a paper with red pencil, trying to stay within the margins and be helpful but not unkind, I throw it down on the floor when the phone rings. Can we come to Sunday brunch across town? Will I bring a salad? I have no time at Christmas, no time at all.

So I try to think of the cut-glass bowls. I put Christmas carols on the hi-fi ("Play 'Rudolph the Red-Nosed Reindeer' again, Mommy") and sit down to examine my own priorities. What do I want out of Christmas? What does it mean to me at the heart of the rustling tissue paper, blinking lights, ringing phone? What must I find time to do? As I listen to the familiar carols, my mind begins to clear. I realize first that Christmas means, oddly enough, silence. At Christmas I feel more than ever a need to get away from myself, from others, and listen to the quiet. I find myself taking long walks after dark, walking by my neighbors' houses, looking at their trees blazing in the windows, admiring the cheerful displays on their outdoor evergreens. I listen to the crackle of frosty branches in the wind, the crunch of my footsteps on the ice, my own moist breath as I puff into a wool scarf with the faint smell of mothballs.

On a cold, bright night when the stars are out above the city, and the remaining elms on our street cast strange dark patterns on the white snow, it seems to me while I walk that I can listen to passing time. I can almost hear the year slipping by. I don't much like New Year's Eve; I stay home in indignant protest against being automatically forced to stay up until midnight. . . . But at Christmas I do my thinking about the coming year, and I watch the old one go. Perhaps because we often remember past Christmases, their hopes and disappointments, our childhoods stretching out behind us, we can have at Christmas an uncanny sense of where we are and where we may be going. I always feel a little sad, recalling past losses and failures, but then I think of what we celebrate at Christmas, a birth and a new beginning, and I am comforted. I can almost feel hope in the air and see it sparkle in the lighted trees. As I step back into my warm little house, I don't feel so cross. I have another chance. Next year maybe I will do better. . . .

Perhaps as part of my wish to reaffirm bonds at Christmas, I also make some time in my kitchen, baking special treats to share with others. I study glossy pictures in magazines, clip recipes, read them to myself at night in bed. If I didn't have a full-time job, I fantasize, I could spend the whole month creating gingerbread houses, turning out dozens of decorated cookies, rush from door to door with loaves of swirled, candied beraised bread. As it is I usually have to settle for one long Saturday morning surrounded by spotted, yellowing recipes never used, cake flour that seems a suspicious antique gray; fancy molds dug out from the cobwebbed corners. Last year it was plum pudding, from scratch, with as many jeweled fruits as I could stuff into the batter—three plum puddings actually, since my molds were rather small. We ate one Christmas Day, gave one away to friends to take home, shared another with neighbors later in the week. For days after the actual baking smells were gone, an aroma of warmth and sweetness seemed to linger in my kitchen.

I am always tired from Christmas. Sometimes I get cranky, catch cold, come down with a headache; signs of stress, I do not need to be told. It may be foolish to try to cram so much into an already bursting schedule, to sandwich concerts around exams to be graded, plum pudding between cards to be answered, a long walk under starlight when presents are waiting to be wrapped. But I cannot bring myself to give up any more of Christmas than I am absolutely forced to. I fervently pack it all in as my sister and I stuffed those glass dishes into my Mother's stretching nylons so many Christmases ago. Like my mother, I want to set out the tokens of love on the living room floor, look past their gaudy color and cut-glass gleam, ignore the ruined stockings that held them, and remember why they are there.

Till Eight

GARNETT ANN SCHULTZ

It seems that Christmas morning
Takes the longest time to come,
As though the hours will never pass
To say the night is done.
However hard we try to sleep,
We're still so wide awake;
But Mom so very firmly states,
"You can't get up till eight."

We listen in our tiny beds
And wish the hours away,
Just waiting for the mantel clock
To tell it's Christmas Day.
It should be Christmas morning now,
It seems so very late;
But all our pleading ends the same:
We'll have to wait till eight.

Now Mom and Dad don't understand
How quiet we could be
And not disturb their sleep at all
Just playing noiselessly.
I'm sure that Santa wouldn't mind
The little peek we'd take.
It's really such a waste of time
To have to sleep till eight.

It seems to me that grown-up folks
Make such an awful fuss;
You'd think they'd be more curious
And anxious just like us,
Instead of sticking to the rules
On such a special date.
It seems a million years somehow,
On Christmas morn . . . till eight.

Santicipation

ALICE LEEDY MASON

It was Christmas Eve and Santa
Soon would bring our gifts and toys.
We were waiting in our bunkbeds
Like good little girls and boys.

Then a "thump" beside the fireplace
Brought us out in nothing-flat!
We know that it was Santa . . .
He left without his hat.

WRAPPING AND UNWRAPPING

BEN LOGAN

$\mathcal{I}$n our Christmas preparations, as though there was some need to maximize confusion, all the present-wrapping was done on Christmas Eve. The children took over the upstairs landing which was soon knee-deep in presents, wrapping paper, and spools of ribbons that kept uncoiling even when no one was touching them.

We could hear the chaos. "Where are the scissors? What did you do with the double-stick tape? Who took the labels?" and then the sound of someone thrashing through the wrapping paper in search. The cry, "Get out of here!" meant the cat had joined them.

Kristine once decided to wrap all her presents and put the labels on after. By then she had forgotten which was which and had to unwrap most of them.

BEAUTIFULLY WRAPPED PRESENTS EMERGED AND WERE CARRIED DOWN TO BE PLACED UNDER THE TREE.

Roger liked to disguise his gifts. A phonograph record for Suzanne could not just be wrapped. That was too obvious. When he finished, he had hidden it inside a mannequin of a private investigator, using pillows, my old London Fog trench coat, and my fishing hat pulled down over a plastic bowl with a face painted on it.

Suzanne was the neatest, less a captive of the chaos. She carefully guarded her own scissors. She was suspected of hoarding all the plastic bows that had never been used before, yet was delighted with colored tissue paper that had been left near an open window and was patterned by the rain.

Despite the disaster area left behind on the landing, beautifully wrapped presents emerged and were carried down to be placed under the tree. Then we gathered in the living room; and Jacqueline served cranberry juice, because it was a Christmas color, and banana bread that had been buttered and then placed for a few minutes under the broiler.

Carols were playing. An ancient wind-up music box, which had a turning

Photograph © William H. Johnson

wooden tree with holders for tiny candles, played "Silent Night" and every few bars turned itself off with a loud click. The candles on the Christmas tree were lighted. I watched them carefully as my father had watched, though there was progress. He had stood with a bucket of water, just in case. I had

*T*HROUGH SOME CONTINUING INSANITY, THERE WAS ALWAYS AT LEAST ONE TOY THAT HAD TO BE ASSEMBLED.

placed a fire extinguisher at the end of the sofa.

A small glass of cranberry juice and a cookie were put on the hearth for Santa. Stockings were hung. The music box clicked a last time. Taking turns with a candle snuffer, we put out the candles on the tree, the wicks holding pinpoints of light for a moment, then winking out and sending little spirals of smoke up toward the star and the light from the kerosene lamp.

Then to bed—the children only, of course. Much was left to be done. Through some continuing insanity, there was always at least one toy that had to be assembled. Once it was an Irish Mail pedal car for Roger with instructions that might have made more sense to someone building a dirigible. Holes in the metal tubing did not match with other holes, and there was noisy improvising with an electric drill. Always, at least one nut or bolt was missing. Or had the cat taken it? She liked things that clattered and would carry small objects to the top of the stairs and push them down, step by step.

Jacqueline and I still had present wrapping to do, first making certain all doors to children's rooms were closed. Next, restore the landing to order. As we picked up and smoothed out wrapping paper, the lost scissors, tape, ribbons, and bows came back to the surface. Once, we found the missing labels in the refrigerator.

Finally, to bed, then up again to go down and drink part of Santa's juice and take a bite from his cookie. We forgot it one year. The juice was untouched but a mouse had remembered to nibble the cookie.

The rest is like looking into a kaleidoscope of memory again, morning always coming too early for parents who had been assembling toys and wrapping things at two AM. The sky lightened, and from the children's rooms came loud, time-to-get-up noises that were supposed to sound accidental.

"Stay upstairs," we yelled, and went down to launch the day. I started a fire in the living-room fireplace and lighted the candles in three old Mexican branding irons that stood on the mantel. The door to the living room was kept closed, the children on the stairs now, edging down step by step, the dog sitting with them, barking.

Jacqueline came from the kitchen, carrying a tray with banana bread and hot cocoa. We lighted the Christmas tree candles and the lamp with the reflector. I put "Joy to the World" on the record player, opened the living-room door, and that was the signal for a rush down the stairs. The rush stopped just inside the living-room door. The children stood there for a moment, staring around the room that was lighted only by the candles, the fireplace, and the small kerosene lamp, as though

wanting to preserve that collective image of Christmas morning.

Santa Claus presents, not wrapped because that was another tradition, were in plain sight, but the children carefully did not see them right away. They went first to the bulging stockings, pulling out Red Delicious apples, nuts, candies, little gifts such as whistles and nerve-shattering clickers, and sometimes magical chocolate oranges that were encased in foil, each section neatly separable.

Eyes had been turning toward the Santa presents, and now they went to them and vanished from the group for a time, exploring the one pres-

ent that had seemed most important in pre-Christmas discussions.

I sat on the floor by the tree, handing out presents one by one, youngest child first. Everyone else watched and waited for the unveiling and the response. Often the gift was passed around for others to hold and see.

Then, the next present.

That meant the gift-giving lasted a great part of Christmas Day, the living room slowly acquiring a carpet of crumpled wrappings which could not be picked up because the cat so enjoyed running at and burying herself in the paper.

Photograph © Jessie Walker

O Christmas Tree

TRADITIONAL | GERMAN TRADITIONAL

on - ly green when sum - mer's here, But

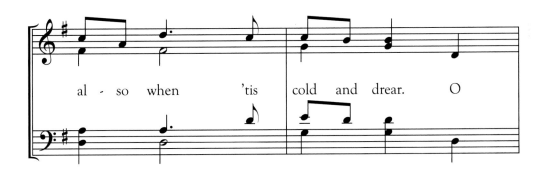

al - so when 'tis cold and drear. O

Christ - mas Tree! O Christ - mas Tree! Thy

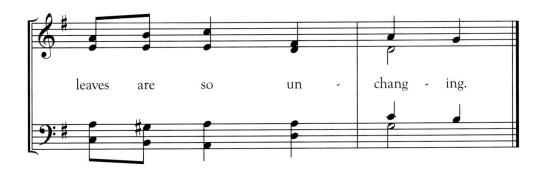

leaves are so un - chang - ing.

Photograph © Jessie Walker

Merry Christmas

AUTHOR UNKNOWN

In the rush of the merry morning,
When the red burns through the gray,
And the wintry world lies waiting
For the glory of the day,
Then we hear a fitful rushing
Just without upon the stair,
See two white phantoms coming,
Catch the gleam of sunny hair.

Are they Christmas fairies stealing
Rows of little socks to fill?
Are they angels floating hither
With their message of goodwill?
What sweet spell are these elves weaving,
As like larks they chirp and sing?
Are these palms of peace from heaven
That these lovely spirits bring?

Rosy feet upon the threshold,
Eager faces peeping through;
With the first red ray of sunshine,
Chanting cherubs come in view.
Mistletoe and gleaming holly,
Symbols of a blessed day,
In their chubby hands they carry,
Streaming all along the way.

Well we know they never weary
Of this innocent surprise;
Waiting, watching, listening always
With full hearts and tender eyes,
While our little household angels,
White and golden in the sun,
Greet us with the sweet, old welcome—
"Merry Christmas, everyone!"

Under the Tree

MARGARET RORKE

Under the tree on Christmas Day,
Ribboned in colors rich and gay,
Sit the surprises bought and made,
Waiting the hour of loving trade.

Under the tree the random stack
Lies as it fell from Santa's pack.
Each little gift will play its part.
Each is to please a child at heart.

Under the tree 'tis plain to scan
All of the time it took to plan
What would delight and furnish cheer
So's to make merry this time of year.

Under the tree we share the joy
Born with the birth of one small Boy,
Born and reborn in God's design
Under the tree—the faithful pine.

THE
Spirit
OF
CHRISTMAS

Christmas is the season for kindling the
fire of hospitality in the hall, the genial
flame of charity in the heart.

WASHINGTON IRVING

THE INSIDE OF CHRISTMAS

LUCILLE CRUMLEY

*T*he outside of Christmas is everywhere to see. It is in the lighted and glittering Christmas tree, in holly wreaths on a door, and in red candles in the window. It is in a hundred toys in gaily decorated shop windows, in gifts wrapped in bright paper and colored ribbons and tinsel.

The outside of Christmas can be heard all over America, in music floating out over the air from shopping centers, radios, and television; in carols sung by children, in chimes and organ music; in the voices of church choirs and in sleigh bells. The outside of Christmas can be tasted too. Tasted in the turkey and oyster dressing and cranberry sauce and pies and cakes and cookies and family dinners and "open house."

In the rush and hurry of the Christmas season, many limit their contacts to the outside of Christmas only. They are so busy that they have no time left to get inside of Christmas; so the holy season becomes a surface experience and not a spiritual existence. To find the true riches of the season, we must penetrate the surface glitter and get inside to the heart of Christmas.

I have found it by my fireside in my home—I have felt the inflow of goodwill and joy and peace. I have found the great light of the manger story. I have found it under the stars on a cold winter night as I walked in the falling snow. I have found it at the bedside of a sleeping child that I loved, as I thought about the miracle of children. I have found it at the beginning of a new day when the household had not yet awakened to the activity of Christmas gaiety. I have found it in the singing of young children who had love and faith in their hearts.

The inside of Christmas is everywhere, wanting to enter and make its glory known. Take the time to quiet the heart and ease the mind. "Seek and ye shall find" the inside of Christmas, and your soul will glow with a new radiance akin to the Star of Bethlehem.

> THE INSIDE OF CHRISTMAS IS EVERYWHERE, WANTING TO ENTER AND MAKE ITS GLORY KNOWN.

Historic Round Church, Richmond, Vermont. Photograph © William H. Johnson

Light of the World

Donna Arlynn Frisinger

Heaven knelt to kiss the earth, so goes the age-old story.

And darkness could not foil the grand displaying of His glory,

Beginning with the wonder-star that shone down on His face:

The grand marquee that sparked the world to hunger after grace.

Amidst the frenzied searching, growing, never-ending lists,

The human soul again responds—there must be more than this:

The shopping malls, last-minute sales, Salvation Army ringing. . . .

A still, small voice that fuels the quest for purpose and for meaning,

As crystal white and rainbow globes illuminate man's plight,

Like twinkling stars they're strung to sing a glory-song tonight.

From rooftop's outlined blinking ropes, to firefly-christened trees,

Cascading strings of icicles, and sparkling evergreens,

They glow from windows, soaring steeples, softly pointed gables

To script a birthday card to Him, born lowly in a stable,

Dazzling small-town village streets and towering city heights:

A gypsy dance of whirling, twirling, swirling Christmas lights!

Still legions try to quell the ray of hope this season brings,

Yet every decoration shouts the triumph of our King!

For love-light wrapped in newborn skin one night in Bethlehem:

The final, brilliant, radiant Word—at God's own bold "Amen."

THE GIFT

MARILYN KOETZ

I don't want a thing for Christmas," Aunt Agatha said, sternly, "not a thing. Do I make myself clear?"

"But Aunt Agatha, you know Dan and I will get you something," I cajoled. "After all, you're his favorite aunt."

Her rigid posture and frosty expression told me I had gone too far. I knew she had interpreted my intended-to-be-kind remark as patronizing.

"How old are you, Kathleen?" she asked.

"Twenty."

"And exactly how long have you and my nephew Daniel been married?"

"Seven months and thirteen days . . ."

"Spare me the hours and minutes." (Did I detect the faintest glimmer of a smile?) "You are new to this family. I am extremely fond of Daniel. Nevertheless, there is not one thing I need or want. Don't waste your time or money on a gift for me."

I could feel myself blushing. "I—I don't know what to say."

"You needn't say anything. I don't mean to be unkind, just explicit. Will you have more tea?"

"No, thank you." Embarrassed, I stood up. To cover my confusion, I pretended to be engrossed in drawing on my thick wool gloves. "I really stopped by to invite you over for Christmas Eve," I said hopefully. (I would win over this austere woman.) "Since Dan and I moved to Grandfather's farm, we have lots of room to entertain. I love everything about that house! There are so many rooms, and the walnut woodwork is beautiful."

"I'm pleased you're so fond of Papa's home. I grew up there, so there are many memories."

"Living there gives Dan and me a sense of family."

> *I* REALLY STOPPED
> BY TO INVITE
> YOU OVER FOR
> CHRISTMAS EVE,"
> I SAID HOPEFULLY.

"The family appreciates Daniel and you acting as caretakers. . . ."

There was an awkward silence. After a few seconds I cleared my throat. "You haven't said you'll come Christmas Eve."

"Christmas Eve. Yes, well . . . This year, you see . . ."

Nervously, I looked out the window at the softly falling snowflakes. Suddenly my Christmas spirit overwhelmed me. "*Please* come, Aunt Agatha. We especially want you to come. Really! No one can take your place with us."

"Why, thank you, Kathleen. Then I'd be delighted to come—if you're really sure you want me this year." Suddenly she was warm and friendly.

"Oh, we do, we do! I've always loved Christmas, and this year it will be especially memorable at the farm. We have a candle in every window, and there's room for a huge tree in the front bay window."

She smiled. "It is a remarkable place, isn't it? Especially during the holidays. And now, what shall I bring: my whiskey cake or my Irish soda bread? . . . Oh, I'll just bring both."

"Why, thank you, Aunt Agatha."

She walked me to the door, and to my astonishment, delivered a cool kiss to my cheek. "I'll see you on Christmas Eve, then. About what time?"

"Seven. We thought we'd have the tree and gifts first and then a late Christmas Eve supper."

"That's our family tradition," she said with satisfaction as she closed the door behind me.

Snow was falling in slow motion—beautiful,

lazy flakes that settled, cozy as a quilt, on the chilled landscape. I got in my car humming "White Christmas." I always looked forward to this season above all others, and this year I had a new husband, a new home, and a whole new family to make things even merrier. I was eager to meet all Dan's relatives. Because we had married in my hometown—fifteen hundred miles away from Dan's—only his parents, two sisters, and their families had attended the wedding. Now, during the holidays, I would get to know the relatives I'd only met casually since our marriage.

The car radio was playing "Silent Night," and the car's tires were crunching deliciously through accumulating snowdrifts. I didn't have a glimmer of the disaster I had just set in motion.

Just one more stop—at Aunt Violet's—and then I'd go home and make Dan a big pot of chili.

Aunt Violet took a few minutes to answer the door. "Why, hello, Kathleen. Are you having trouble with the sweater you're knitting for Daniel?"

"I did bring it, Aunt Violet," I said as she led me to the big Queen Anne chair in her living room.

THIS YEAR I HAD A NEW HUSBAND, A NEW HOME, AND A WHOLE NEW FAMILY TO MAKE THINGS EVEN MERRIER.

"Would you mind checking to see if you can find my mistake?"

She put on her glasses, took the sweater from me, and expertly went over my work. . . .

"Would you like something to eat or drink?"

"No thanks." How she could make those knitting needles fly! "I'm going home to make chili. I just stopped by to tell you that Dan and I are having Christmas Eve this year. Won't it be lovely at the farmhouse? You *will* come, won't you Aunt Violet?"

"Of course I will, dear. I want to see Dan's face when he opens this sweater! He doesn't even know I taught you to knit. Oh, and I always bring my cranberry relish and sweet pickle slices. . . ."

Later that evening, Dan and I sat beside a crackling apple-wood fire eating chili. . . .

"So what did my beautiful young wife do today—besides make mouth-watering chili?"

"I worked on your Christmas present. Oh Dan, I can't wait to give it to you!"

"What color is it, Kathy? Is it bigger than a bread box?"

"You could never, ever guess what it is, even with clues. Oh, and I went shopping, and then I called on Aunt Agatha and Aunt Violet and invited them both for Christmas Eve."

"You *what?*" Dan put down his bowl and stared at me.

I was puzzled by his tone. "What in the world's the matter with you? I invited them to Christmas Eve dinner. Why are you so excited?"

"Kathy, they haven't spoken to each other for eleven years!"

"No!" Now it was my turn to be startled.

"How on earth could you do such a thing? I can't believe it."

"But Dan," I protested, "I didn't know. No one ever told me."

"How could you be a member of this family for seven months and not know? You've met them both. Surely we must have mentioned . . ."

"No one told me, Dan! I could never forget a thing like that."

"Well, what did Aunt Agatha say? What did Aunt Violet say? Weren't they upset when you told them they were both invited?"

"They both said 'yes.' I didn't specifically mention to either of them that I'd invited the other. I told each of them we were having Christmas Eve this year. They both know that means the whole family."

"No way! They come on alternating years. This year it's Aunt Violet's turn. She's expecting to come. I can't believe Aunt Agatha accepted. Are you sure you didn't misunderstand her?"

"She's bringing her whiskey cake and Irish soda bread."

"She is coming. I can't believe it. She couldn't have gotten the impression that Aunt Violet won't be here, could she?"

"I don't see how . . . Oh Dan, oh darling!" I suddenly remembered urging Aunt Agatha to come, telling her no one could take her place. No wonder she had become so warm and friendly. She thought that I had deliberately excluded Aunt Violet because I preferred her company on Christmas Eve. I explained to Dan, ending with, "What should we do?"

"I have no idea what you should do. . . . Why don't you call my mother in the morning? Maybe she can suggest something. She's tried to get the aunts together for years. The holidays are always so hard on Dad with the aunts feuding. Maybe she'll have an idea—but I doubt it."

Wonderful. My first faux pas as Dan's wife would ruin Christmas for my new family. And just when I'd been feeling so married, so adult.

I phoned Dan's mother as soon as he'd left for work the next morning. I explained the situation and held my breath.

"Oh Kathy, I'm so sorry we let you in for this. I can't imagine how we could have forgotten to tell you about the aunts. I guess we've all become so used to the situation we don't think about it anymore. Oh dear! Oh my! And they are both coming, you say?"

"Couldn't they both come?" I asked. "There are thirty-two people invited, with all the cousins and their children. Maybe I could keep them separated somehow."

My mother-in-law is tactful. "Well, I don't know, Kathy. Do you think you could?"

Of course I couldn't. The farmhouse is large, but we would all be together in the parlor and dining room for the festivities. "Oh, I could just cut my heart out!" I moaned.

She laughed in sympathy. "That seems a bit dramatic. Unfortunately, the only suggestion I can offer is that you tell Agatha the truth."

"But how can I? She thinks I asked her especially. I hate to hurt her like that."

"Maybe you could tell Violet then."

"But it's her turn," I said, trying not to whine. "That would be cruel. What did they get so mad about it the first place?"

"It was such a little thing, really. As a matter of fact, it was our family Christmas Eve celebration that started it. Violet was having the family that year. She's the artsy-craftsy one, so she hand-painted little invitations and mailed them. I talked to Agatha on the telephone that Christmas Eve afternoon and mentioned how attractive the little cards were. Agatha said she hadn't received one. I said, 'Well, you two talk on the phone every day. You helped her plan the dinner. Why would she think she needed to send you a mailed invitation?' I didn't think any more about it. That night though, Agatha didn't come. I told Violet why Agatha was so upset, so she called her. It had never occurred to Violet to send her sister a written invitation. Agatha was deeply offended. She said, 'You have one sister and one brother. Did you send your brother an invitation?' Violet said 'Well, yes, but he has a family.' Agatha banged down the phone, and they haven't spoken since."

"And now I've gone and brought it all back up again. Just tell me what you think I should do, and I'll do it," I said desperately.

"Kathy dear, I think the only thing you can do is tell Agatha exactly what happened. She knows it's Violet's year to come. She may be hurt, but it's the only solution I can think of. Do you think you can handle it?"

"I'll have to." *Please, please offer to call Aunt Agatha for me!*

After a few seconds she said, "Would you like me to call Agatha for you?"

I couldn't believe my ears when I heard myself say, "Thank you, but I think it's my responsibility."

She seemed relieved. "Well, it's only twenty days until Christmas. I wouldn't wait too long."

The next day I put Christmas music on the stereo and baked cookies. It was gray and cold and windy outside. Inside, the farmhouse was warm and cozy and smelled of cinnamon. It was nineteen days until Christmas—quite a long time, really. Tomorrow I would call Aunt Agatha.

The days before the holidays were hectic. I finished Dan's sweater. I scrubbed the wood floors in the parlor and polished the furniture. The house smelled of lemon oil. Dan's mother phoned to ask if I'd talked to Aunt Agatha yet. It was fifteen days until Christmas, and it had slipped my mind. I said I'd call her tomorrow for sure. . . .

One week before Christmas—seven days. I called all the relatives to check on who was bringing what. I addressed and mailed a card to everyone who had sent us one but who had not been on our list. I wrapped gifts while I hummed Christmas carols. Everything was right on schedule.

Three days before Christmas I awakened to the sound of sleet on the roof. After breakfast I took the turkey out of the freezer to thaw. I made the sauce for the baked ham. I decided to make yeast rolls from my mother's recipe. I listened to "Here Comes Santa Claus" on the radio. The weather forecast promised new snow for the holidays. There was really only one thing that still needed attention—one thing that I kept shoving to the back of my mind. And now, two days before Christmas Eve, my stomach churned as it stared me in the face.

Tomorrow I would go see Aunt Agatha in person and throw myself on her mercy. I could put it off no longer. It must be done. Last chance!

On Christmas Eve morning it was snowing. The world was white and glistening, the house fragrant with the smell of evergreens. The stately tree in the parlor was surrounded by gifts wrapped in gold, green, and white, with magnificent red bows. The candy dishes were filled with homemade fudge. As I roasted hazelnuts in the oven, I thought of my new red-velvet dress hanging in the closet upstairs. I knew tonight it would contrast vividly with my stark white, completely bloodless face. I had not contacted Aunt Agatha. It was too late. I tried to put it out of my mind. It was too late. There was nothing I could do now.

Christmas Eve. The snow is exquisite. The farmhouse smells of roasting ham, baking turkey, Christmas pine, and burning apple wood. Aunt Violet and Dan's sisters and their families are here early to help. The children are starry-eyed and angel-perfect in their Christmas clothes. I have on my red dress, and I'm wearing the only-for-special-occasions Worth perfume that Dan loves. Aunt

Violet comes in from the kitchen. She has taken off her apron.

"Everything's ready in the kitchen, Kathleen. Now it's my job to answer the front door."

"Oh, it's so cold, Aunt Violet. I'll do it."

"Nonsense! This is my job," she says firmly.

Dan looks at my face. He thinks I'm upset because I want to play hostess. "This is Kathy's first Christmas, Aunt Violet. Why don't you both welcome the new arrivals?"

The doorbell rings. I race Aunt Violet to the door. Dan's parents come in, loaded with packages. We kiss. We hug. We go to the parlor. Dan has Christmas music on the stereo. If ever there was a seemingly perfect, Christmas-card Christmas, it is here, now, in this place.

The doorbell rings a short, imperative blast. The very sound says "Aunt Agatha!" I think my heart has stopped. I arrive at the door just as Aunt Violet puts her hand on the knob. She opens the door. Aunt Agatha stands there holding her wrapped whiskey cake on a silver platter. The beribboned Irish soda bread is tucked under her arm.

The aunts stare at each other. They stare at me. I am stone and ice in my red dress. There is no movement, no sound. It seems as if the whole world has stopped. In the corner of my eye, I see the family gathering.

I look at Aunt Violet. Then at Aunt Agatha. My knees are shaking. Then, faintly I hear the strains of "Hark the Herald Angels Sing" coming from the stereo. Suddenly I blurt out, "Peace on earth!"

Both aunts stand totally still. The sounds of the carol float through the door. Suddenly Aunt

Agatha drops the cake and bread just as Aunt Violet steps forward.

"Sister!" Aunt Agatha sobs as she throws her arms around Aunt Violet.

"Agatha!" Aunt Violet is weeping and embracing her sister at the same time.

Then the whole family surrounds them and everyone is laughing and crying and hugging and kissing. The stereo is now playing "Oh, Come, All Ye Faithful," and the children begin running through the house, wild with excitement.

Dan comes to put his arm around me with a strangely soft expression in his eyes. He puts his face next to me and inhales my perfume as he nuzzles my cheek. "Now, Kathy," he whispers in my ear, "you know perfectly well that Aunt Agatha told you *not* to get her a gift for Christmas."

Keeping Christmas

KAY HOFFMAN

Deck the house with cedar boughs,
And hang the mistletoe;
Trim the tree with baubles bright
And little lights that glow.

Keep the Yule log brightly burning;
Fill each stocking to the rim;
Enjoy the warm traditions
That the Yuletide ushers in.

But set aside a time each day
To pray and to recall
The deeper Christmas meaning,
Most precious part of all.

Reread the sacred Scriptures
Of that holy, wondrous night
When God sent the little Christ-Child
To guide men's paths aright.

May traditions warm of Yuletide,
Fill your home and heart with cheer;
May the little Christ Child's coming
Guide your pathway through the year.

Roasted Turkey with Rich Turkey Gravy

1 turkey, 14 to 16 pounds (thawed, if frozen)
Salt and black pepper
Cornbread Stuffing (page 153), optional
¼ cup butter, melted

1 cup water
4 to 5 cups turkey or chicken broth
½ cup unsalted butter
¾ cup all-purpose flour

Position oven rack at lowest level. Preheat oven to 325°F. Remove neck and giblets from turkey cavity. Rinse turkey inside and out with cold water. Pat dry. Generously rub body and cavity with salt and pepper. Stuff if desired. Place turkey, breast side up, on rack in large roasting pan. Brush outside of turkey with ¼ cup melted butter. Cover loosely with foil, and roast about 2¼ to 3½ hours if not stuffed, 2¾ to 4 hours if stuffed. Remove foil for last 30 to 45 minutes of cooking time to brown skin. Thigh meat will register 175°F to 180°F when done (stuffing should be at least 165°F), and juices should run clear when pierced with a knife. Remove from oven, transfer to serving dish, cover loosely with foil, and let rest 20 minutes before carving.

Pour pan juices through a fine-mesh sieve into a large measuring cup. Skim off and discard fat; set aside. Straddle roasting pan across 2 burners; add water and bring to a boil over high heat, stirring and scraping up brown bits, approximately 1 minute. Strain into measuring cup containing pan juices. Transfer juices to a large bowl and add enough broth to bring total up to 6 cups; set aside. In a 4-quart heavy pot, melt ½ cup unsalted butter and whisk in flour to make a roux. Cook roux over medium heat, whisking constantly, 5 minutes. Add broth mixture in a slow, continual stream, whisking vigorously to prevent lumps. Bring to a boil, stirring occasionally. Stir in any juices accumulated on serving platter and simmer 5 minutes. Season to taste with salt and pepper.

Carve turkey and serve with gravy. Makes 12 to 14 servings.

Whipped Sweet Potatoes with Honey

4 large sweet potatoes (about 4 to 5 pounds)
½ cup butter, room temperature

2 tablespoons honey, or more to taste
Salt and black pepper

Preheat oven to 350°F. Pierce sweet potatoes all over with fork. Bake potatoes for 1½ hours or until very soft. Remove potatoes from oven and let stand until cool enough to handle. Peel potatoes and place flesh in mixing bowl; add butter. Using an electric mixer, beat until fluffy and smooth. Mix in 2 tablespoons of honey. Season to taste with salt and pepper and more honey by the teaspoonful, if desired. Transfer sweet potatoes to serving bowl. Sweet potatoes can be made ahead and reheated in an 8 x 8-inch baking dish. Makes 8 servings.

Cornbread Stuffing with Fresh and Dried Fruit

⅓ cup butter
1½ cups chopped onions
1½ cups chopped unpeeled McIntosh or
   Golden Delicious apples
1 cup chopped celery with leaves

10 pitted prunes, diced
10 dried apricot halves, diced
   Salt and black pepper
8 ounces seasoned cornbread stuffing
1 cup chicken broth

Preheat oven to 375°F. In large heavy skillet over medium heat, melt butter. Add onions and sauté until translucent, about 10 minutes. Add apples and celery; sauté until celery begins to soften, about 10 minutes. Scrape contents of skillet into large bowl. Add prunes and apricots. Season with salt and pepper to taste; toss. Add stuffing and toss until evenly combined. Add broth and toss well. Transfer stuffing to greased 8 x 8-inch baking dish. Bake, covered, about 15 minutes. Uncover and bake until heated through and top begins to form crust, about 15 additional minutes. Makes 8 to 10 servings.

SPIRIT OF CHRISTMAS

L. JUNE STEVENSON

The rustle of wrap and the bustle of activity was a mystery of Christmas. When did Mother purchase and wrap all those presents that ended up under the tree? Where did she hide them from the curious eyes of eager children? Only a sudden furtive cover up of something on her chair or a hand behind her back told us that something was up. One year, I searched the house, finally to spy a wrapped package in the rafters of the basement. Its long handle suggested it was a new snow shovel, something I really didn't want. Imagine my joy on Christmas morning when out came a popcorn popper!

Self-centered as we were, we knew that Christmas was about giving as well as receiving. Some gifts were made with all the pride and confidence that the recipient would appreciate the time, effort, and love that went into the making. Mother always helped. She bought celluloid kewpie dolls, those chubby dolls with topknots, at the five-and-dime store, cut a hole in the back and let me fill them with talcum powder. Together we dressed and wrapped them to give to my favorite lady teachers.

I WAS LEARNING ABOUT THE GIVING OF GIFTS FROM THE HEART.

We scoured ads and shopped carefully for bargains, those precious finds of crystal or china, miraculously marked down for the first wise consumer to spot. Maple fudge was stirred and beaten to a smooth gloss, dates were pressed between colored vanilla icing, then packed into chocolate boxes, saved from earlier occasions. I was learning about the giving of gifts from the heart.

Then, there were the gifts that caused some distress to the giver. Though I was too young to go along, I heard my parents talk about delivering baskets to the "less fortunate." The concern and sadness in their voices was obvious as they described the conditions they encountered.

Somehow I understood that these people were part of our Christmas too, like all the others on the fringes of society that I have encountered since.

Today I knit throughout the year mittens in all sizes, caps, and scarves as Mother did, never forgetting that there are those among us who don't have a warm home and a loving family.

My childish mind sensed there was something profound about Christmas that went far beyond gifts, glitter, and greed. The mystery of the season lay not in the presentation of gifts but in the giving of self to a love that was beyond understanding. That jolly old man in a red suit was just the beginning of a lifetime of study and searching. The spirit of Christmas was embodied in the opening of self to the wonder of that love, given to humankind on the first Christmas—a love incarnate, a lasting, living memory. Mother, Christmas, and love. What more can I say?

Photograph © Jessie Walker

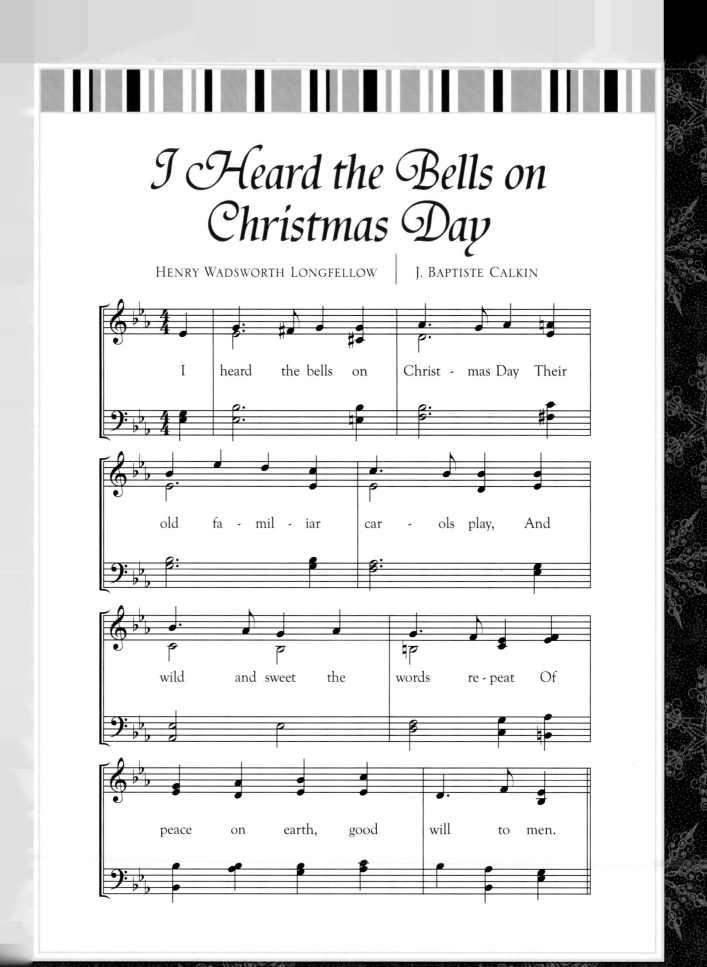

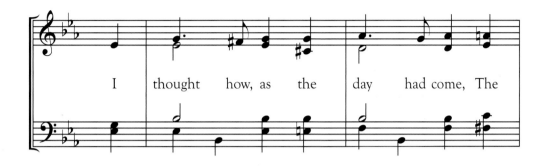

I thought how, as the day had come, The

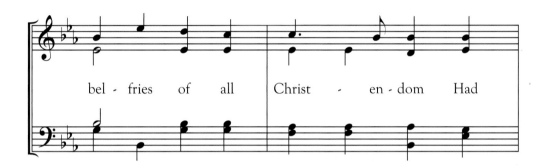

bel - fries of all Christ - en - dom Had

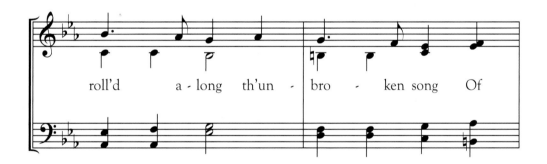

roll'd a - long th'un - bro - ken song Of

peace on earth, good will to men.

God Bless Us All

MARGARET E. SANGSTER

God bless us all! With Tiny Tim
'Tis thus we finish prayer and hymn,
While cheerily from lip to lip
The Christmas wishes gaily trip;
God bless us all, the circle round
Wherever are our dear ones found;
At home, abroad, please God, we say,
God bless His own on Christmas Day!

God bless the golden heads arow
Where ruddy hearth flames leap and glow;
God bless the baby hands that clasp
Heart fibers in their clinging grasp;

God bless the young with eager gaze;
God bless the sage of lengthened days;
At home, abroad, please God, we cry,
God guard His own, 'neath any sky!

God ease the weary ones who bear
A cumbering weight of grief and care;
God give the wage no ill can spoil,
The honest loaf for honest toil;
We sound the heartfelt prayer and hymn,
And breathe "Amen" with Tiny Tim,
As reverently, please God, we say,
God bless us all on Christmas Day!

—w—

Keep the Christmas Spirit

MILDRED L. JARRELL

If we keep the Christmas spirit
Not for one special day,
But hold its meaning in our hearts
All year to give away;

Share love and joy and kindness,
So all the world will know
The beauty of the message
Of Christ's birth so long ago.

If we keep the Christmas spirit,
The world will live anew;
And we will reap rich blessings
In all we say and do.

For Christmas is the peace we find
When giving love to others,
And it returns to each of us
When men reach out as brothers.

INDEX

The Greatest Gift

The Greatest Gift

Julie K. Hogan, EDITOR

IDEALS PUBLICATIONS
NASHVILLE, TENNESSEE

An Ideals Treasury of Christmas
ISBN-13: 978-0-8249-5910-4

Published by Ideals Publications
A Guideposts Company
Nashville, Tennessee
www.idealsbooks.com

Previously published as *The Greatest Gift*, copyright © 2002

Printed and bound in the USA

Publisher, Patricia A. Pingry
Art Director, Eve DeGrie
Designer, Marisa Calvin
Copy Editor, Lisa Ragan
Permissions, Patsy Jay
Book Editor, Julie K. Hogan

Library of Congress CIP data on file

ACKNOWLEDGMENTS

BALDWIN, FAITH. "Christmas Is in the Unexpected Gift" from
Many Windows, Seasons of the Heart. Copyright © 1958 by Faith
Baldwin Cuthrell. "Christmas" from *The Christian Herald,*
December 1949. Used by permission of Harold Ober
Associates. *(Acknowledgments continued on page 160.)*

The Greatest Gift

The Gift *of* Christmas Spirit

CHRISTMAS-GIVING AND CHRISTMAS-LIVING

Henry Van Dyke

The custom of exchanging presents on a certain day in the year is very much older than Christmas and means very much less. It has been obtained in almost all ages of the world and among many different nations. It is a fine thing or a foolish thing, as the case may be; an encouragement to friendliness or a tribute to fashion; an expression of good nature or a bid for favor; an outgoing of generosity or a disguise of greed; a cheerful old custom or a futile old farce, according to the spirit which animates it and the form which it takes.

But when this ancient and variously interpreted tradition of a day of gifts was transferred to the Christmas season, it was brought into vital contact with an idea which must transform it, and with an example which must lift it up to a higher plane. The example is the life of Jesus. The idea is unselfish interest in the happiness of others.

Not that it must all be solemn and serious. For the most part it deals with little wants, little joys, little tokens of friendly feeling. But the feeling must be more than the token; else the gift does not really belong to Christmas.

It takes time and effort and unselfish expenditure of strength to make gifts in this way. But it is the only way that fits the season.

The finest Christmas gift is not the one that costs the most money but the one that carries the most love. . . .

But how seldom Christmas comes—only once a year; and how soon it is over—a night and a day! If that is the whole of it, it seems not much more durable than the little toys that one buys of a fakir on the street corner. They run for an hour and then the spring breaks and the legs come off, and nothing remains but a contribution to the dust heap.

But surely that need not and ought not to be the whole of Christmas. . . . If every gift is the token of a personal thought, a friendly feeling, an unselfish interest in the joy of others, then the thought, the feeling, the interest, may remain after the gift is made.

The little present, or the rare and long-wished-for gift . . . may carry a message something like this:

"I am thinking of you today, because it is Christmas, and I wish you happiness. And tomorrow, because it will be the day after Christmas, I shall still wish you happiness; and so on, clear through the year. I may not be able to tell you about it every day, because I may be far away; or because both of us may be very busy; or perhaps because I cannot even afford to pay the postage on so many letters or find the time to write them. But that makes no difference. The thought and the wish will be here just the same. In my work and in the business of life, I mean to try not to be unfair to you or injure you in any way. In my pleasure, if we can be together, I would like to share the fun with you. Whatever joy or success comes to you will make me glad. Without pretense, and in plain words, goodwill to you is what I mean, in the Spirit of Christmas."

It is not necessary to put a message like this into high-flown language, to swear absolute devotion and deathless consecration. In love and friendship, small, steady payments on a gold basis are better than immense promissory notes. Nor, indeed, is it always necessary to put the message into words at all, nor even to convey it by a tangible token. To feel it and to act it out—that is the main thing.

There are a great many people in the world whom we know more or less, but to whom for various reasons we cannot very well send a Christmas gift. But there is hardly one, in all the circles of our acquaintance, with whom we may not exchange the touch of Christmas life.

In the outer circles, cheerful greetings, courtesy, consideration; in the inner circles, sympathetic interest, hearty congratulations, honest encouragement; in the inmost circle, comradeship, helpfulness, tenderness.

> Beautiful friendship tried by sun and wind
> Durable from the daily dust of life.

After all, Christmas-living is the best kind of Christmas-giving.

Everywhere, Everywhere, Christmas Tonight
Phillips Brooks

Everywhere, everywhere, Christmas tonight!
Christmas in lands of the fir-tree and pine,
Christmas in lands of the palm-tree and vine,
Christmas where snow peaks stand solemn and white,
Christmas where cornfields stand sunny and bright.

Christmas where children are hopeful and gay,
Christmas where old men are patient and gray,
Christmas where peace, like a dove in his flight,
Broods o'er brave men in the thick of the fight;
Everywhere, everywhere, Christmas tonight!

For the Christ-child who comes is the Master of all;
No palace too great, no cottage too small;
The angels who welcome Him sing from the height,
"In the city of David, a King in His might."
Everywhere, everywhere, Christmas tonight!

Then let every heart keep its Christmas within,
Christ's pity for sorrow, Christ's hatred for sin,
Christ's care for the weakest, Christ's courage for right,
Christ's dread of the darkness, Christ's love of the light.
Everywhere, everywhere, Christmas tonight!

So all the stars of the midnight which compass us round
Shall see a strange glory and hear a strange sound,
And cry, "Look! the earth is aflame with delight,
O sons of the morning, rejoice at the sight."
Everywhere, everywhere, Christmas tonight!

The chimneys of peace on the roofs of snow keep watch, and the world is still.
—Esther M. Wood

CHRISTMAS AND PETER MOSS

Mary Small

The waste ground close to the water's edge belonged to the Harbour Trust. Except for the gulls, it was no good for anything.

Nearby, partly hidden by trees, stood a small stone cottage. Peter Moss lived there. Once he had been a ship's engineer and had traveled all over the world . . . a long time ago.

The cottage was old, much older than Peter Moss. His grandfather had built it back in the early days. Many times the council had tried to buy it to make way for new buildings, but it was not for sale. Peter Moss often wondered what would happen to it when he died. He had no family, only Bosun, his dog.

Every day, Peter Moss and Bosun walked down to the waste ground for exercise. Bosun was young and full of energy. He loved to chase the stones and sticks that his master threw for him. When the old man grew tired, he would stand leaning on his stick gazing across the water to the tall, skyscraper buildings of the city. Sometimes a container ship would pass on its way to the docks and there were always ferries coming and going. Peter Moss reckoned

that he had the best view in the city. Yet, in spite of the bustle around him, he was lonely.

Every other day, except Sunday, Peter Moss made the long, slow walk to the shops at the top of Clark Street to buy groceries. It always alarmed him to see the bulldozers busy so near to his home and more and more flats rising up to the sky, full of new people. No one took any notice of the old man; they were too busy, too worried about their own affairs.

"Christmas gets earlier and earlier every year!" Peter Moss muttered as he looked in the shop windows. It was the time of the year he dreaded the most, for he was a shy man and although he had money, it could not buy him friends.

One Saturday morning he was surprised to see three youngsters with bikes walking around the waste ground talking together. They stayed there a long time and then went away.

On Sunday, more children came. They seemed very excited about something. They took spades and started to dig up the ground. Peter Moss stood at the window watching. He didn't like to interfere but they had no right to intrude. He waited a while, then opened the door and walked down with Bosun.

"What are you doing?" he asked. "This land belongs to the Harbour

Trust. You can't dig it up like that."

"Why not?" said Glen, the biggest boy. "It's not used for anything."

"We need somewhere to ride our bikes," said Nikos.

"The street's no good," said Werner, punching the ground with the heel of his boot.

"You'll get into big trouble if you do anything with it," said Peter Moss.

"But we want to make a practice track with dips and jumps," said Michelle. "For that we need rough ground. This couldn't be better."

All the youngsters stood and stared at him. Peter Moss didn't know what to do. "You'll have to find somewhere else," he said gruffly. Not wanting to argue, he called to Bosun and started to walk away. He could feel their strong resentment.

The youngsters muttered among themselves.

"There isn't anywhere!" shouted Glen angrily.

Peter Moss stopped. The children were right; for them there was nowhere. Youngsters nowadays didn't have the space he had when he was a boy.

"Watch it!" said Glen. "Old Nosey-Parker's coming back!"

Spades in their hands, they stood and waited.

"I've just had a thought," said Peter Moss. "I'm on the Harbour Trust Board Committee. You leave the ground alone and I'll have a talk to them and maybe to the council too."

"Okay by us," said Glen. "When will you know?"

"That I can't say," said Peter Moss. "You'll have to be patient. Come back and see me later this week. I live in the cottage up there."

The boys were at school when the people from the Harbour Trust came. They spent a long time looking at the land and a long time talking to Peter Moss. Then they went away. The old man felt sad. They hadn't made a decision, one way or the other. He knew that if the children didn't get the land they'd blame it on him and go elsewhere.

"This thing takes time," he said when the children knocked on the door.

Just when he had almost given up hope, the telephone rang. As Peter Moss listened to the voice, a big smile spread over his face.

"The kids will be delighted," he said. "Yes, I'll be only too pleased to keep an eye on things. I'm sure there'll be no trouble."

So the children dug ditches and made jumps and a track for their BMXs.

As the days grew longer, the old man had company most evenings and all the weekends. It was impossible for him to be lonely. When they weren't riding, the children would sit on the veranda and talk to him.

"When I was young, they didn't make bikes like that," said Peter Moss in amazement as Werner shot out from a ditch and twisted his bike in the air, and Nikos and Glen bounced over the Whoopy-doos.

"They're very expensive," said Elke. "Gino and Francesco who live next to us are selling newspapers to buy them."

"My brothers Jose and Mario are getting them for Christmas," said Rosa, "but you mustn't tell. It's a secret."

"Nikos hopes to trade his for a better one," said Sofie.

"No way can I get one," said Richard. "My dad's out of work."

"Nor I," said Paul. "We haven't the money."

From the conversations, Peter Moss was surprised that so many of the children living in the street came from different countries, places he knew quite well from his years at sea; Nikos and Sofie from Greece, Werner and Elke from Germany, Gino and Francesco from Italy, Jose, Mario, and Rosa from South America, Michelle from France, Danny and Kate from England. He heard about Tuan and Khai who had come from Vietnam in an open boat.

"They live over the shop next to the Chinese restaurant," said Kate. "They seem very poor and can't speak much English."

Peter Moss started to do a lot of thinking.

The Friday before Christmas, a white panel van pulled up at his house. When it had gone, Peter Moss went up the street to the hardware store. He bought a piece of shipboard, a small tin of paint and a brush. Then he went home and locked the door. He was busy all day.

Danny was the first to notice the sign hung on the veranda.

"Look!" he said, calling to the others. "BMX BIKES FOR HIRE, NO CHARGE. Say! What has the old man done?"

Dropping their bikes, the children raced up to the cottage and banged on the door. Bosun barked as Peter Moss opened it.

"Happy Christmas!" he said. "Come in and see!"

They crowded inside and there in a back room stood four brand new bikes.

"For anyone who needs one," said Peter Moss. "I asked for the best in the shop."

"They're sure good!" said Michelle. "Look, snake-belly tires, chrome-moly frames and all!"

Talking excitedly, the children jostled each other to hold the bikes.

"It's unreal!" said Glen. Thanks a million. Wait'll we tell the others."

Next evening, the children called a meeting at Werner's and Elke's house.

"What do you think he does at Christmastime?" they said.

"Probably nothing much."

On Christmas Eve, Peter Moss went to the shops early to buy food for himself and Bosun.

The waste ground lay silent and empty that evening. Peter Moss had just sat down to tea when Bosun growled softly. There was a noise of feet shuffling on the veranda, then suddenly voices started singing.

Peter Moss went to the door and opened it. There stood Nikos and Sofie and all their Greek friends. Peter Moss had never heard a song so beautiful.

"Happy Christmas, Mr. Moss!" sang out Rosa, and the carol singers moved aside so that her brothers Jose and Mario could carry a Christmas tree into the house. They placed it in a corner of the kitchen and the visitors crowded round, covering it with goodies and decorations.

"Our dad reckoned you'd need some good cheer," said Danny and Kate, putting a gift under the tree.

"And I bought a new collar for Bosun," said Richard.

"And I've brought him biscuits," said Paul.

"You must eat this tonight," said Elke, placing a cake braided and covered with icing on the table. "We call it a *stollen*. Gino and Francesco have some-

thing for you too," and the Italian boys came forward with a dish full of delicious looking toffee.

"It's *torrone*," said Gino, "made from almonds and sugar and honey."

"You're invited to dinner at our place tomorrow," said Glen and Donna.
"We'll fetch you at midday."

"We must hurry," said Rosa, "for we have our dinner tonight after church."

"We have ours too!" said Francesco.

Peter Moss sat down in his chair at the table. He looked at the children
and the bright things around him. There were tears in his eyes.

"Thank you," he said very softly. "It's the most wonderful Christmas I've
ever had."

Good King Wenceslas

JOHN MASON NEALE

LATIN SPRING CAROL

1. Good King Wen-ces - las look'd out On the Feast of
2. "Hith - er, page, and stand by me, If thou know'st it
3. "Bring me flesh, and bring me wine, Bring me pine - logs
4. "Sire, the night is dark - er now, And the wind blows
5. In his mas-ter's steps he trod, Where the snow lay

Ste - phen, When the snow lay round a - bout,
tell - ing, Yon - der peas - ant, who is he?
hith - er, Thou and I will see him dine,
strong - er; Fails my heart, I know not how,
dint - ed; Heat was in the ver - y sod

Deep and crisp and e - ven; Bright - ly shone the moon that night,
Where and what his dwell-ing?" "Sire, he lives a good league hence,
When we bear them thith-er." Page and mon-arch forth they went,
I can go no long-er." "Mark my foot-steps, my good page,
Which the saint had print-ed. There-fore, Chris-tian men, be sure,

Tho' the frost was cru - el, When a poor man
Un - der-neath the moun-tain; Right a - gainst the
Forth they went to - geth-er; Through the rude winds'
Tread thou in them bold - ly: Thou shalt find the
Wealth or rank pos - sess-ing, Ye who now will

came in sight, Gath - 'ring win - ter fu - el.
for - est fence, By Saint Ag - nes' foun - tain."
wild la - ment And the bit - ter weath - er.
win - ter's rage Freeze thy blood less cold - ly."
bless the poor, Shall your-selves find bless - ing.

CAROLS IN THE COTSWOLDS

Laurie Lee

The week before Christmas, when snow seemed to lie thickest, was the moment for carol singing; and when I think back to those nights it is to the crunch of snow and to the lights of the lanterns on it. Carol singing in my village was a special tithe for the boys; the girls had little to do with it. Like haymaking, blackberrying, stone clearing, and wishing people a happy Easter, it was one of our seasonal perks.

So as soon as the wood had been stacked in the oven to dry for the morning fire, we put on our scarves and went out through the streets, calling loudly between our hands, till the various boys who knew the signal ran out from their houses to join us. One by one they came stumbling over the snow, swinging their lanterns round their heads, shouting and coughing horribly.

"Coming carol barking then?"

We were the Church Choir, so no answer was necessary. For a year we had praised the Lord out of key, and as a reward for this service we now had the right to visit all the big houses, to sing our carols and collect our tribute.

To work them all in meant a five-mile foot journey over wild and generally snowed-up country. So the first thing we did was to plan our route; a formality, as the route never changed. All the same, we blew on our fingers and argued; and then we chose our leader. This was not binding, for we all fancied ourselves as leaders, and he who started the night in that position usually trailed home with a bloody nose.

Eight of us set out that night. There was Sixpence the Simple, who had never sung in his life (he just worked his mouth in church); the brothers Horace and Boney, who were always fighting everybody and always getting the worst of it; Clergy Green, the preaching maniac; Walt the Bully; and my two brothers.

As we went down the lane other boys, from other villages, were already about the hills, bawling "Kingwenslush," and shouting through keyholes "Knock on the knocker! Ring at the bell! Give us a penny for singing so well!" They weren't an approved charity as we were, the choir; but competition was in the air.

Our first call as usual was the house of the Squire, and we trooped

nervously down his drive. For light we had candles in marmalade jars suspended on loops of string, and they threw pale gleams on the towering snowdrifts that stood on each side of the drive. A blizzard was blowing but we were well wrapped up, with army puttees on our legs, woolen hats on our heads, and several scarves round our ears. As we approached the Big House across its white silent lawns, we too grew respectfully silent. The lake nearby was stiff and black, the waterfall frozen and still. We arranged ourselves shuffling round the big front door, then knocked and announced the choir.

A maid bore the tiding of our arrival away into the echoing distances of the house, and while we waited we cleared our throats noisily. Then she came back, and the door was left ajar for us, and we were bidden to begin. We brought no music; the carols were in our heads. "Let's give 'em 'Wild Shepherds',"said Jack. We began in confusion, plunging into a wreckage of keys, of different words and tempos; but we gathered our strength; he who sang loudest took the rest of us with him, and the carol took shape, if not sweetness.

This huge stone house, with its ivied walls, was always a mystery to us. What were those gables, those rooms and attics, those narrow windows veiled by the cedar trees? As we sang "Wild Shepherds" we craned our necks, gaping into the lamplit hall which we had never entered; staring at the muskets and untenanted chairs, the great tapestries furred by dust—until suddenly, on the stairs, we saw the old Squire himself standing and listening with his head on one side.

He didn't move until we'd finished; then slowly he tottered toward us, dropped two coins in our box with a trembling hand, scratched his name in the book we carried, gave us each a long look with his moist blind eyes, then turned away in silence. As though released from a spell we took a few sedate steps, then broke into a run for the gate. We didn't stop till we were out of the grounds. Impatient, at last, to discover the extent of his bounty, we squatted by the cow sheds, held our lanterns over the book, and saw that he had written "Two Shillings." This was quite a good start. No one of any worth in the district would dare to give us less than the Squire.

So with money in the box, we pushed on up the valley, pouring scorn on each other's performance. Confident now, we began to consider our quality and whether one carol was not better suited to us than another. Horace, Walt said, shouldn't sing at all; his voice was beginning to break.

Steadily we worked through the length of the valley, going from house to house, visiting the lesser and the greater gentry—the farmers, the doctors, the merchants, the majors, and other exalted persons. It was freezing hard and blowing too; yet not for a moment did we feel the cold. The snow blew into our faces, into our eyes and mouths, soaked through our puttees, got into our boots, and dripped from our woolen caps. But we did not care. The collecting box grew heavier, and the list of names in the book longer and more extravagant, each trying to outdo the other.

Mile after mile we went, fighting against the wind, falling into snowdrifts, and navigating by the lights of the houses. And yet we never saw our audience. We sang, as it were, at the castle walls.

As the night drew on there was trouble with Boney. "Noel," for instance, had a rousing harmony which Boney persisted in singing, and singing flat. The others forbade him to sing it at all, and Boney said he would fight us. Picking himself up he agreed we were right, then he disappeared altogether. He just turned away and walked into the snow and wouldn't answer when we called him back. Much later, as we reached a far point up the valley, somebody said "Hark!" and we stopped to listen. Far away across the fields from the distant village came the sound of a frail voice singing, singing "Noel," and singing it flat—it was Boney, branching out on his own.

We approached our last house high up on the hill, the place of Joseph the farmer. For him we had chosen a special carol, which was about the other Joseph, so, that we always felt that singing it added a spicy cheek to the night. The last stretch of country to reach his farm was perhaps the most difficult of all. In these rough bare lanes, open to all winds, sheep were buried and wagons lost. Huddled together, we tramped in one another's footsteps, powdered snow blew into our screwed-up eyes, the candles burned low, some blew out altogether, and we talked loudly above the gale.

Crossing, at last, the frozen millstream—whose wheel in summer still turned a barren mechanism—we climbed up to Joseph's farm. Sheltered by trees, warm on its bed of snow, it seemed always to be like this. As always it was late; as always this was our final call. The snow had a fine crust upon it, and the old trees sparkled like tinsel. We grouped ourselves round the farmhouse porch. The sky cleared, and broad streams of stars ran down over the valley and away to Wales. On Slad's white slopes, seen through the black sticks of its woods, some red lamps still burned in the windows.

Everything was quiet; everywhere there was the faint crackling silence of

the winter night. We started singing, and we were all moved by the words and the sudden trueness of our voices. Pure, very clear, and breathless we sang:

> As Joseph was a-walking
> He heard an angel sing,
> 'This night shall be the birth-time
> Of Christ the Heavenly King.
> He neither shall be borned
> In Housen nor in hall,
> Nor in a place of paradise
> But in an ox's stall.'

And two thousand Christmases became real to us then; the houses, the halls, the places of paradise had all been visited; the stars were bright to guide the Kings through the snow; and across the farmyard we could hear the beasts in their stalls. We were given roast apples and hot mince pies, in our nostrils were spices like myrrh, and in our wooden box, as we headed back for the village, there were golden gifts for all.

Each year, old carols are sung for a few. It's part of our gift beginning anew. The Christmas story never can end, for dear Jesus lives in the hearts of our friends.
—*Author Unknown*

Christmas Prayer
Ralph Spaulding Cushman

Let not our hearts be busy inns
That have no room for Thee
But cradles for the living Christ
And His nativity.

Still driven by a thousand cares,
The pilgrims come and go;
The hurried caravans press on;
The inns are crowded so!

Here are the rich and busy ones,
With things that must be sold;
No room for simple things within
This hostelry of God.

Yet hunger dwells within these walls,
These shining walls and bright,
And blindness groping here and there
Without a ray of light.

Oh, lest we starve, and lest we die
In our stupidity,
Come, Holy Child, within and share
Our hospitality.

Let not our hearts be busy inns
That have no rooms for Thee
But cradles for the living Christ
And His nativity.

The Joy of Christmas
John Greenleaf Whittier

Somehow, not only for Christmas
But all the year through,
The joy that you give to others
Is the joy that comes back to you;
And the more you spend in blessing
The poor and lonely and sad,
The more of your heart's possessing
Returns to make you glad.

Let There Be Christmas
Author Unknown

So remember while December
Brings the only Christmas day,
In the year let there be Christmas
In the things you do and say.
Wouldn't life be worth the living,
Wouldn't dreams be coming true
If we kept the Christmas spirit
All the whole year through?

Christmas Gifts
Alberta Dredla

Of all the gifts that Christmas brings,
The best are made of little things:
Melody of carols all the year;
Cheer to friends that you hold dear;
Courage to someone else to start
Some task for which he hasn't heart;
Thoughts for those with less than you;
Faith though the future's not in view;
Fun and laughter to go everywhere;
Kindness to show how much you care;
Strength to begin all over again;
And love to seek the best in every man.
While other seasons come and go
And another year hurries past,
Let's give again the little things—
They are the gifts that last.

Now not a window small or big
But wears a wreath or holly sprig.
—*Rachel Field*

The Keeper of the Inn

William P. Remington

There is an old story about the keeper of the inn, who owned the stable where Jesus was born. The census was being taken by Caesar Augustus; roads were crowded with people going to their own cities and the Inn at Bethlehem was full to overflowing. For one thing Marcus Publius, a great man of Rome with his servants and his horses, his scribes and his guards, filled the place. The old Innkeeper was kept hurrying hither and yon and even then could not do all the things demanded of him. And all the time more travelers were coming and asking that they might abide there for the night.

There was One who came the next morning, whom the Innkeeper would not have turned away for all the silver in the world, if only he had known who He was. There were two of them, a man, who might have been a carpenter or a potter, and his wife sitting all doubled up upon a donkey.

The man said his wife was ill and could travel no farther. But the Innkeeper grew angry at his pleas, shouting at him, "Can I make more rooms arise by striking my staff upon the ground?" And so the Innkeeper missed the greatest opportunity that ever an Innkeeper had. Long years afterwards it never did much good to repeat over and over again, "They were but poor folk and how was I to know?" When afterwards the Child Jesus was born in the stable and a great light filled all the heavens and there was a sound of heavenly music, Marcus Publius and his servants were still in a drunken sleep, and the Innkeeper had missed his great chance.

So it had been, and so it will be for many throughout the ages. Always there is that light in the heavens, that song in the air, that bright star, clear in the Eastern sky, which tell of the Birth of Christ. He comes to all and yet only a few see the light and run joyfully to the manger-cradled King.

We each one are the Keepers of the Inn. Never were there so many people on the roads demanding an entrance to our hearts and homes.

You Merry Folk
Geoffrey Smith

You merry folk, be of good cheer,
For Christmas comes but once a year.
From open door you'll take no harm
By winter if your hearts are warm.
So ope the door and hear us carol
The burthen of our Christmas moral.
Be ye merry and make good cheer,
For Christmas comes but once a year;
Scrape the fiddle and beat the drum,
And bury the night ere morning come.

Home for Christmas
Minnie Klemme

The folks are coming home for Christmas.
All the windows are aglow;
We have a tree and wreaths and candles,
And we have some snow!

There are gifts upon the mantel
And there are gifts beneath the tree;
The whole house is breathing Christmas
And so by now are we.

Do I hear sleigh bells in the distance?
We're waiting from cellar to dome.
Hurrah, hurrah, a merry Christmas—
The folks are finally home!

We gathered all our packages and climbed aboard the train, and off to Grandmama's we went at Christmastime again. —Marguerite Gode

THE FIR TREE

Hans Christian Andersen

Most children have seen a Christmas tree, and many know that the pretty and pleasant custom of hanging gifts on its boughs comes from Germany; but perhaps few have heard or read the story that is told to little German children, respecting the origin of this custom. The story is called "The Little Stranger" and runs thus: In a small cottage on the borders of a forest lived a poor laborer, who gained a scanty living by cutting wood. He had a wife and two children who helped him in his work. The boy's name was Valentine, and the girl was called Mary. They were obedient, good children, and a great comfort to their parents. One winter evening, this happy little family was sitting quietly round the hearth, the snow and the wind raging outside, while they ate their supper of dry bread, when a gentle tap was heard on the window, and a childish voice cried from without, "Oh, let me in, pray! I am a poor child with nothing to eat and no home to go to, and I shall die of cold and hunger unless you let me in."

Valentine and Mary jumped up from the table and ran to open the door, saying, "Come in, poor little child! We have not much to give you, but whatever we have we will share with you."

The stranger-child came in and warmed his frozen hands and feet at the fire, and the children gave him the best they had to eat, saying, "You must be tired, too, poor child! Lie down on our bed; we can sleep on the bench for one night."

Then said the little stranger-child, "Thank God for all your kindness to me!" So they took their little guest into their sleeping-room, laid him on the bed, covered him over, and said to each other, "How thankful we ought to be! We have warm rooms and a cozy bed, while this poor child has only heaven for his roof and the cold earth for his sleeping-place."

When their father and mother went to bed, Mary and Valentine lay quite contentedly on the bench near the fire, saying, before they fell asleep, "The stranger-child will be so happy tonight in his warm bed!"

These kind children had not slept many hours before Mary awoke, and softly whispered to her brother, "Valentine, dear, wake and listen to the sweet music under the window."

Then Valentine rubbed his eyes and listened. It was sweet music indeed, and sounded like beautiful voices singing to the tones of a harp:

> O holy Child, we greet thee! bringing
> Sweet strains of harp to aid our singing.
> Thou, holy Child, in peace art sleeping,
> While we our watch without are keeping.
> Blest be the house wherein thou liest,
> Happiest on earth, to heaven the nighest.

The children listened, while a solemn joy filled their hearts; then they stepped softly to the window to see who might be without.

In the east was a streak of rosy dawn, and in its light they saw a group of children standing before the house, clothed, in silver garments, holding golden harps in their hands. Amazed at this sight, the children were still gazing out of the window when a light tap caused them to turn around. There stood the stranger-child before them, clad in a golden dress, with a gleaming radiance round his curling hair. "I am the little Christ child," he said, "who wanders through the world bringing peace and happiness to good children. You took me in and cared for me when you thought me a poor child, and now you shall have my blessing for what you have done."

A fir tree grew near the house; and from this he broke a twig, which he planted in the ground, saying, "This twig shall become a tree and shall bring forth fruit year by year for you."

No sooner had he done this than he vanished and with him the little choir of angels. But the fir-branch grew and became a Christmas tree, and on its branches hung golden apples and silver nuts every Christmastide.

Such is the story told to German children concerning their beautiful Christmas trees, though we know that the real little Christ child can never be wandering, cold and homeless, again in our world, inasmuch as he is safe in heaven by his Father's side; yet we may gather from this story the same truth which the Bible plainly tells us that anyone who helps a Christian child in distress, it will be counted unto him as if he had indeed done it unto Christ himself. "Inasmuch as ye have done it unto the least of these, my brethren, ye have done it unto me."

As Ye Do It unto These

Author Unknown

In little faces pinched with cold and hunger
Look, lest ye miss Him! In the wistful eyes
And on the mouths unfed by mother kisses,
Marred, bruised, and stained, His precious image lies!
And when ye find Him in the midnight wild,
Even in the likeness of an outcast child,
O wise men, own your King!
Before His cradle bring
You gold to raise and bless,
Your myrrh of tenderness,
For "As ye do it unto these," said He,
"Ye do it unto Me."

A Kindled Flame of Love

Edgar A. Guest

When it's Christmas, man is bigger
   And is better in his part;
He is keener for the service
   that is prompted by his heart.
All the petty thoughts and narrow
   seem to vanish for awhile
And the true reward he's seeking
   is the glory of a smile.
Then for others he is toiling
   and somehow it seems to me
That at Christmas he is almost
   what God wanted him to be.

Christmas is the season for kindling the fire of hospitality in the hall, the genial flame of charity in the heart.

—*Washington Irving*

The Christmas Guest

Author Unknown

It happened one day near December's end,
Two neighbors called on an old-time friend,
And they found his shop so meager and mean,
Made gay with a thousand boughs of green.
And Conrad was sitting with face a-shine
When he suddenly stopped as he stitched a twine.

And said, "Old friends, at dawn today
When the cock was crowing the night away,
The Lord appeared in a dream to me
And said, 'I am coming your guest to be.'
So I've been busy with feet astir
Strewing my shop with branches of fir.

The table is spread and the kettle is shined
And over the rafters the holly is twined.
And now I will wait for my Lord to appear
And listen closely so I will hear
His step as he nears my humble place
And I open the door and look on his face."

So his friends went home and left Conrad alone,
For this was the happiest day he had known.
For long since his family had passed away
And Conrad had spent many a sad Christmas Day.
But he knew with the Lord as his Christmas guest,
This Christmas would be the dearest and best.

So he listened with only joy in his heart,
And with every sound he would rise with a start
And look for the Lord to be at the door
Like the vision he had a few hours before.
So he ran to the window after hearing a sound,
But all he could see on the snow-covered ground

Was a shabby beggar whose shoes were torn
And all of his clothes were ragged and worn;
But Conrad was touched and went to the door,
And he said, "Your feet must be frozen and sore—
I have some shoes in my shop for you,
And a coat that will keep you warmer, too."

So with grateful heart the man went away,
But Conrad noticed the time of day;
He wondered what made the dear Lord so late
And how much longer he'd have to wait
When he heard a knock and ran to the door,
But it was only a stranger once more—

A bent old lady with a shawl of black,
With a bundle of kindling piled on her back.
She asked for only a place to rest
But that was reserved for Conrad's great guest,
But her voice seemed to plead, "Don't send me away,
Let me rest for a while on Christmas Day."

So Conrad brewed her a steaming cup
And told her to sit at the table and sup.
But after she left, he was filled with dismay,
For he saw that the hours were slipping away,
And the Lord had not come as he said he would
And Conrad felt sure he had misunderstood.

When out of the stillness he heard a cry,
"Please help me and tell me where am I."
So again he opened his friendly door
And stood disappointed as twice before.
It was only a child who had wandered away
And was lost from her family on Christmas Day.

Again Conrad's heart was heavy and sad
But he knew he could make this little girl glad.
So he called her in and wiped her tears
And quieted all her childish fears,
Then he led her back to her home once more,
But as he entered his own darkened door,

He knew that the Lord was not coming today
For the hours of Christmas had passed away.
So he went to his room and knelt down to pray,
And he said, "Lord, why did you delay,
What kept you from coming to call on me,
For I wanted so much your face to see."

When soft in the silence, a voice he heard,
"Lift up your head for I kept my word.
Three times my shadow crossed your floor,
Three times I came to your lowly door;
For I was the beggar with bruised cold feet;
I was the woman you gave something to eat,

And I was the child on the homeless street.
Three times I knocked, three times I came in,
And each time I found the warmth of a friend.
Of all the gifts, love is the best;
I was honored to be your Christmas Guest."

God Rest Ye Merry, Gentlemen

TRADITIONAL ENGLISH

1. God rest ye mer - ry, gen-tle-men, Let noth-ing you dis - may,
2. From God our Heav'n-ly Fa - ther, A bless-ed an-gel came;
3. "Fear not,then," said the an - gel, "Let noth-ing you af - fright,
4. The shep-herds at those ti - dings Re - joic-ed much in mind,
5. And when they came to Beth-le-hem Where our dear Sav-iour lay,

Re - mem-ber Christ our Sav - iour Was born on Christ-mas day,
And un - to cer - tain shep - herds Bro't ti - dings of the same:
This day is born a Sav - iour Of a pure Vir - gin bright,
And left their flocks a - feed - ing, In tem-pest, storm and wind:
They found Him in a man - ger, Where ox - en feed on hay;

The Time Has Come

Poor Robin's Almanack

Now that the time has come wherein

Our Saviour Christ was born,

The larder's full of beef and pork,

The granary's full of corn.

As God hath plenty to thee sent,

Take comfort of thy labors,

And let it never thee repent,

To feast thy needy neighbors.

Old Christmas Returned

Author Unknown

All you that to feasting and mirth are inclined,

Come here is good news for to pleasure your mind,

Old Christmas is come for to keep open house,

He scorns to be guilty of starving a mouse:

Then come, boys, and welcome for diet the chief,

Plum-pudding, goose, capon, minced pies, and roast beef.

The holly and ivy about the walls wind

And show that we ought to our neighbors be kind,

Inviting each other for past-time and sport,

And where we best fare, there we most do resort;

We fail not of victuals, and that of the chief,

Plum-pudding, goose, capon, minced pies, and roast beef.

All travellers, as they do pass on their way,

At gentlemen's halls are invited to stay,

Themselves to refresh, and their horses to rest,

Since that he must be Old Christmas's guest;

Nay, the poor shall not want, but have for relief,

Plum-pudding, goose, capon, minced pies, and roast beef.

The Gift of Love

A Greeting of Love

Fra Giovanni

There is nothing I can give you which you have not; but there is much, very much that, while I cannot give it, you can take. No heaven can come to us unless our hearts find rest in today. Take heaven! No peace lies in the future which is not hidden in the present. Take peace!

The gloom of the world is but a shadow. Behind it, yet within our reach, is joy. Take joy! There is radiance and glory in the darkness could we but see, and to see, we have only to look. I beseech you to look.

Life is so generous a giver, but we, judging its gifts by the covering, cast them away as ugly, or heavy, or hard. Know the covering, and you will find beneath it, a living splendor, woven of love, by wisdom, with power.

And so, at this Christmas time, I greet you. Not quite as the world sends greetings, but with profound esteem and with the prayer that for you, now and forever, the day breaks and the shadows flee away.

A Christmas Prayer

Robert Louis Stevenson

Loving Father, help us remember the birth of Jesus, that we may share in the song of the angels, the gladness of the shepherds, and the worship of the wise men. Close the door of hate and open the door of love all over the world. Let kindness come with every gift and good desires with every greeting. Deliver us from evil by the blessing which Christ brings and teach us to be merry with clear hearts. May the Christmas morning make us happy to be Thy children, and the Christmas evening bring us to our beds with grateful thoughts, forgiving and forgiven, for Jesus' sake. Amen!

PRAYER AT CHRISTMAS

Pat Corrick Hinton

God our Father, it's Christmas at last. Thank you for this big celebration. We are happy because you have given us your greatest gift of love, Jesus your Son. We welcome Jesus and thank you for all the love and hope and peace He brings us. Help us to be like Jesus and bring love and hope and peace to each other. Let the love in our family reach out to everyone we meet today and tomorrow and every day.

Christmas is a golden chain that binds a family in faith, hope, and love . . . drawing each to the open hearth of togetherness.
—Juanita Johnson

The Song and the Star

Grace V. Watkins

My father had the shining gift of song.
His voice was cello-beautiful and strong.
Oh, sometimes, listening to the choir where he
Gave humble, dedicated ministry,
I felt I stood with shepherds, hearing bright
Allegro anthems syllabled with light;
then came with gladness to the manger place
and looked upon the Christ Child's holy face.

My mother had the gift of quietness.
How often her tranquility would bless
My weariness with peace! And in her eyes
It often seemed I saw the star arise
In silent majesty so calm and fair
My heart was filled with wonderment of prayer,
As though that star, more lovely than a gem,
Were leading me to the Child of Bethlehem.

What sweet, what priceless memories they are:
The golden-echoing song, the quiet star!

LATE FOR
CHRISTMAS

Mary Ellen Chase

During those con-
fusing days before
Christmas, while I
wrap gifts for sisters and
brothers, brothers-in-law and
sisters-in-law, nephews and
nieces, aunts and great-aunts,
neighbors and friends, the milk-
man, the postman, the paper
boy, the cook and the cook's
children, the cleaning woman
and the cleaning woman's children, I remember my grandmother, who in the twenty years
I knew her wrapped Christmas
gifts for no one at all. My
grandmother never stood half
submerged in a jungle of silver
cord, gold cord, red ribbon, tinsel ribbon, white tissue paper,
red tissue paper, paper marked
with Aberdeens or angels. She
viewed with fine scorn all such
pre-Christmas frenzy. I remem-
ber her again when my January bills weigh down my desk and my disposition.
My grandmother in all those years never bought a Christmas gift for anyone,
although she gave many. Nor did she make her Christmas gifts by the labor of
her hands, which were almost never idle.

To be sure, she spent most of her waking hours during twelve months of
the year in making gifts, but they were not for Christmas. She made yards
upon yards of tatting, fashioned hundreds of tea cozies, tidies, and table mats,

hem-stitched innumerable handkerchiefs, crocheted fine filet for pillowcases and sheets, knit countless scalloped bands of white lace for the legs of white cotton drawers, and countless stockings, gloves, mittens, scarfs, sacques, and shawls. These creations were all gifts, yet they were never given at Christmas. Instead, they were presented at odd moments to all sorts of odd and sundry persons—to the gardener, the minister's wife, a surprised boy coasting down the hill, the village schoolmistresses, the stage driver, a chance Syrian peddler,

the fishman, the paperhangers, an unknown woman distributing religious literature at the back door, the sexton. Moreover, no one of my grandmother's many acquaintances ever called upon her without departing from her door richer, or at least more encumbered, than when she entered it—nor did my grandmother ever set out empty-handed to return those calls.

My grandmother's nature was essentially dramatic. She loved all sudden, surprising, unexpected things; but she loved them only if either she or God instigated them. Quite illogically she denied this privilege to others. She was distinctly irritated if anyone took her unawares either by a sudden gift or by an unexpected piece of news. She was so filled with life herself that she forever wanted to dispense rather than to receive, to initiate rather than to be initiated.

She loved sudden changes of weather, blizzards, line gales, the excitement of continuous winter cold, northern lights, falling stars; and during many years of her long and abundant life she had had her fill of such abrupt and whimsical behavior on the part of God. For she had spent much of her life at sea, where holidays were mere points in time, unprepared for, often even unnoticed, slipping upon one like all other days, recalled if wind and weather were kind, forgotten if God had other and more immediate means of attracting one's attention to His power and His might. She had spent Christmas in all kinds of strange places: off Cape Horn in a gale; running before the trades somewhere a thousand miles off Africa; in a typhoon off the Chinese coast; in the doldrums, where the twenty fifth of December was but twenty-four still hours in a succession of motionless days; in the bitter cold of a winter storm too near the treacherous cliffs of southern Ireland for comfort or security. Small wonder that she would find it difficult, after her half-reluctant return to village life, to tie up Christmas in a neat parcel and to label it with a date.

As children we were forever asking our grandmother about those Christmases at sea.

"Didn't you give any presents at all, Grandmother? Not to the sailors or even to Grandfather?"

"The sailors," said my grandmother, "had a tot of rum all around in the dogwatch if the weather was fair. That was the sailors' present."

We always smile over "tot." This facetious, trifling word attached to one of such enormity as "rum" in those days of temperance agitation seemed impious to say the least. "What is a tot of rum, Grandmother?"

"A tot," answered my grandmother with great dignity, "is an indeterminate quantity."

"Did the sailors sing Christmas carols when they had the tot?"

"They did not. They sang songs which no child should ever know."

"Then did you and Grandfather have no presents at all, Grandmother?"

"Whenever we got to port we had our presents; that is, if we did not forget that we had had no Christmas. We had Christmas in January or even March. Christmas, children, is not a date. It is a state of mind."

Christmas to my grandmother was always a state of mind. Once she had left the sea, once she was securely on land, where the behavior of God was less exciting, she began to supplement Providence and Fate by engendering excitement in those about her. Her objection to Christmas lay in the fact that it was a day of expectation, when no one could possibly be taken by surprise. She endured it with forbearance, but she disliked it heartily.

Unlike most women of her generation, she cared not a whit for tradition or convention; but she remained to the end of her days the unwilling prey of both. Unlike most women of any generation, she scorned possessions, and she saw to it that she suffered them briefly. We knew from the beginning the fate of the gifts we annually bestowed upon her; yet we followed the admonition and example of our parents in bestowing them. From our scanty Christmas allowance of two dollars each with which to purchase presents for a family of ten, we set aside a generous portion for Grandmother's gift. She was always with us at Christmas and received our offerings without evident annoyance, knowing that what she must endure for a brief season she could triumph over in the days to come.

As we grew older and were allowed at length to select our gifts free from parental supervision, we began to face the situation precisely as it was. Instead of black silk gloves for Grandmother, we chose for her our own favorite perfumery; we substituted plain white handkerchiefs for the black-edged ones which she normally carried; a box of chocolates took the place of one of peppermints; a book called *Daily Thoughts for Daily Needs* was discarded in favor of a story by Anna Katharine Green.

My grandmother waited for a fortnight or longer after Christmas before she proffered her gifts to family, neighbors, and friends. By early January, she concluded, expectation would have vanished and satiety be forgotten; in other words, the first fine careless rapture of sudden surprise and pleasure might again be abroad in the world. She invariably chose a dull or dark day upon which to deliver her presents. Around three o'clock on some dreary afternoon was her time for setting forth. Over her coat she tied one of her stout aprons of black sateen, and in its capacious lap she cast all her own unwanted gifts—a black silk umbrella, odd bits of silver and jewelry, gloves, handkerchiefs, stockings, books, candies, Florida water, underwear, bedroom slippers, perfumeries, knickknacks of every sort; even family photographs were not excluded! Thus she started upon her rounds, returning at suppertime empty-handed and radiant.

I remember how once as children we met her thus burdened on our way home from school.

"You're rather late for Christmas, Grandmother," we ventured together.

"So, my dears, were the Three Wise Men!" she said.

The many days foretold by the preacher for the return of bread thus cast upon the waters have in the case of my grandmother not yet elapsed. For, although she has long since gone where possessions are of no account, and where, for all we know, life is a succession of quick surprises, I receive from time to time the actual return of her Christmas gifts so freely and curiously dispensed. Only last Christmas a package revealed a silver pie knife marked with her initials, and presented to her, I remembered with a start, through the combined sacrificial resources of our entire family fully thirty years before. An accompanying note bore these words:

> Your grandmother brought this knife to my mother twenty-eight years ago as a Christmas gift. I remember how she came one rainy afternoon in January with the present in her apron. I found it recently among certain of my mother's things, and knowing your grandmother's strange ways as to Christmas gifts, I feel that honesty demands its return to you. You may be interested in this card which accompanied it.

Tied to the silver pie knife by a bit of red ribbon obviously salvaged long ago from Christmas plenty was a card inscribed on both sides. On one side was written: "To grandmother with Christmas love from her children and grandchildren" and on the other: "To my dear friend, Lizzie Osgood, with daily love from Eliza Ann Chase."

Go Tell It on the Mountain

JOHN W. WORK JR.   SPIRITUAL

Go,   tell it on the moun - tain,   o - ver the hills and   ev'ry-where;

Go,   tell it on the moun - tain, that Je - sus Christ   is   born.

1. While shep - herds kept their watch - ing o'er
2. The shep - herds feared and trem - bled when,
3. Down in a low - ly man - ger the

si - lent flocks by night, be - hold, thro' - out the
lo! a - bove the earth rang out the an - gel
hum - ble Christ was born, and God sent us sal -

D.C.

heav - ens there shone a ho - ly light.
cho - rus that hailed our Sav - iour's birth.
va - tion that bless - ed Christ - mas morn.

Bethlehem of Judea

Author Unknown

A little child,
    A shining star.
A stable rude,
    The door ajar.

Yet in that place,
    So crude, forlorn,
The Hope of all
    The world was born.

May These Be Your Gifts

Author Unknown

May these be your gifts at Christmas—
Warm hearts and shining faces,
Surrounding you to make your home
The happiest of places.

May these be your gifts at Christmas—
Deep peace and lasting love,
That you will share together
With the ones you're fondest of.

May these be your gifts at Christmas—
The promise of a year
Where everything goes well with you
And those you hold most dear.

A Christmas Hymn

Christina G. Rossetti

Love came down at Christmas,
Love all lovely, Love Divine;
Love was born at Christmas,
Star and Angels gave the sign.

Love shall be our token,
Love be yours and love be mine,
Love to God and all men,
Love for plea and gift and sign.

There's More to Christmas

Author Unknown

There's more, much more, to Christmas
Than candlelight and cheer;
It's the spirit of sweet friendship
That brightens all the year;
It's thoughtfulness and kindness,
It's hope reborn again,
For peace, for understanding
And for goodwill to men!

May you have the greatest two gifts of all on these holidays: Someone to love and someone who loves you. —John Sinor

THE THREE WISE MEN OF TOTENLEBEN

Alexander Lernet-Holenia
Translated by Judith Bernays Heller

*I*n November of the year 1647, the commander-in-chief of the French forces during the Thirty Years War, Marshal Turenne, set out on a long journey. His horsemen picked up two young people who were traveling through the country, poorly clad and on foot. One was a young man, the other a young woman. The woman was pregnant, perhaps already in her seventh or eighth month. Questioned, they replied they were husband and wife, who had been forced to leave the place where they had been living with the wife's parents. They were now on their way to the husband's home—a village called Totenleben on the lower Main River, where they hoped to find living quarters and perhaps some means of livelihood as well.

Marshal Turenne took in only snatches of this. Nevertheless he noted the odd name of the village which was the goal of the young people. He dismissed them, and then reached a decision.

One night he suddenly appeared in the region of the lower Main. Both he and his men were armed and wrapped in warm coats and furs. The moon glistened on their helmets. All the land around was devastated. Preceding the troop by some hundred paces, two horsemen with rifles in their hands stopped now and again in front of a clump of snow-covered bushes or at the ruins of a burned

farm and cried out: "Who goes there?" But there was no one to answer. The whole region lay still as in death. As the cavalcade pressed steadily forward, silver hoarfrost spun its web in the icy ruts.

The riders stopped at the edge of a wood. Turenne dismounted and two henchmen apparently according to orders previously given, approached him and removed his fur coat and hat. The moonlight gleamed on the gold chain he wore around his neck.

Meanwhile, several of his officers had gotten off their horses and approached him while the serving men pulled a garment over his armor. It was a white robe, bespangled with golden stars. They covered his face with a black veil. The whole was the costume for the eve of Twelfth Night, such as waits or carol singers wear. The servants took the pistols from his saddlebag and placed them in his hands.

"I am going now," he said to his officers. "Wait for me here. If I have not returned by three o'clock in the morning, then have the village search for me."

"Yes, your excellency," was the officers' reply. The Marshal departed alone, trudging over the field of snow.

He had walked several hundred paces when the silhouette of a village appeared before him. At its northern boundary a light was shining. Toward this he made his way. The beam came from a peculiar lantern made out of oiled paper in the shape of a star and attached to a pole some eight feet high.

Two men, one of whom carried the pole, stood by the light. They too wore the costume of waits, though the veils they wore were white.

Turenne raised his pistols and stepped up to them as he gave his own name. The two answered, giving their names: "Wrangel," and "Melander." They were, respectively, the commander-in-chief of the Swedes, newly appointed after Torstenson's retirement, and the Supreme Chief of the Imperial Armies, Count Melander of Holzapfel.

All three of them now raised their veils and looked into one another's eyes, then let the veils fall once more over their faces. Turenne hid his pistols under his robe, and said: "I have asked you gentlemen to come here in this disguise so that we may be able to discuss the matters that concern us, undisturbed and in secret. This is the eve of Twelfth Night and we shall be taken for waits. We would do best to proceed to the village to find quarters."

"There is no longer any village," said Melander. "It has been burned to the ground. Your own troops, Count, may have set fire to it."

"Be that as it may," said Wrangel, "we ought to see to it that we find some shelter somewhere. Surely we do not want to stand about here in the cold."

Accordingly they began to move on with their star. Along the village street there were only heaps of rubble where once there had been houses. But near the burned-out church they managed to find a house passably preserved, with its windows boarded up. A faint light shone from between the boards.

They went up to the door and knocked. They had to do this repeatedly before a voice from within inquired what they wanted.

"Open the door," they called, whereupon the door, which no longer had any hinges, was pulled back a bit with a creak. A man stuck his head out.

"What's your business?" he asked.

"We are waits," said Melander. "Let us in."

"Waits?" the man asked. "So early?"

"Yes," said Melander. "Let us in." He crossed the threshold, followed by the two others, after they had put aside the pole with the lantern.

"But look here," said the man, after closing the door behind them, "today is only Christmas Eve."

"No, indeed," said Wrangel, "it's Twelfth Night. Do you people here still go by the old calendar?

The pope has changed the calendar," said Melander. "It was already fourteen days behind, and no longer agreed with the position of the stars. Don't you know that?"

"The village is in ruins," said the man. "The whole countryside is desolate. How should we know whether the pope has changed the calendar or not? We are celebrating Christmas Eve today, if you can still call it celebrating."

"Well," said Wrangel, "never mind. We would like to stay for awhile. Bring us something to eat. We'll pay you in good honest coin."

"I used to be the innkeeper here," said the man, "and my business prospered. But now I have scarcely bread enough for my own family, and if we are thirsty, we have to drink melted snow, for our wells are all stopped up. Sit down, for a seat is all I have to offer. What manner of men are you to believe that you can get alms by singing as waits? Where do you come from? Here, in this village, we are the only ones left alive; and there is not a grain of wheat or a single beast left in the whole region. Everything has been destroyed by the war."

The three commanders looked about them. All they saw was a hearth on which a fire cast its flickering light and a table with a few benches. Smoke filled the room. The innkeeper's wife and a half-grown boy were watching the strangers. In addition, there were two other people in the room—a young man and his young wife. Turenne recognized them as the same two whom he had encountered on his reconnaissance trip.

"Who are they?" he asked in faulty German.

"They are poor people," said the innkeeper, "who came to this place but who could find no shelter anywhere. The man was originally from here; he moved away and got married. But he had to come back, and now I've given them a lodging in the stable. The wife is expecting a child."

"You don't say!" said Turenne. The three strangers sat down at the table.

In the meantime, the others busied themselves near the hearth setting up a Christmas crèche of moss and small wooden figures. They were brightly colored and represented the Holy Family, the angels, the adoring Magi, the shepherds, the ox and the ass. For a while the three generals looked on; then they began their talk. They spoke in French.

"The peace talks that started last year," said Turenne, "are not being conducted in the interest of the armies. If peace were to come, there would be no need to have armed forces. To discuss together what measures should be taken against the conclusion of an overhasty peace is the purpose of my invitation. For even though we are enemies, we are all in the same boat; however you look at it, what's good for one is good for all three of us."

When those who were setting up the crèche heard the talk in a foreign language, they looked over at the three in surprise. For a time the innkeeper listened anxiously, then he approached the table.

"Who are you?" he asked. "You are no ordinary waits. You are foreigners and perhaps soldiers as well. Haven't you convinced yourself hat this country, this village, this house are in ruins and that there's nothing more for you to carry off? What do you want from us? Have you been sent by those who want to take our very lives? That is the only thing you can still take from us."

"Be still," said Melander, "we are the Three Wise Men. We have to discuss something here." And he threw him a golden coin.

The innkeeper looked at the gold piece, for he had not seen its like for many a year. He took it quickly and tested it with his fingers. At the same time, his bearing changed. He wanted to look into the faces of the three, yet his glance could not penetrate their veils. Only now did he notice the boots and spurs visible below their robes, and the metal ends of their leather sword sheaths.

"Your pardon, my lords!" he said, bowing obsequiously, "I would not for the world . . . I did not know . . ."

"Very well, very well," said Melander, "leave us alone."

"May we at least," said the innkeeper, "sing the Christmas song for the gentlemen? It will not disturb you?"

"Sing it, for all I care," said Melander, "but do it quietly."

After some time, those around the crèche began to sing the Christmas song. Toward the end of the song, the young wife stopped singing; she tottered, and clung to her husband. Her pains had begun.

Had it not been for the strangers, the innkeeper would have allowed her to remain in the room and have her baby there. But in the presence of the others he did not dare to do this. The woman was led into the stable where she lay on a pile of moss and dead leaves.

The generals had not noticed when the woman was led out the room. Suddenly the generals appeared to be at odds now, and their voices rose in excitement. It was Melander who pronounced himself most emphatically as against continuation of the war. He said that surely the country was sufficiently desolate, it was plain to see how poverty-stricken the people had become here as

well as elsewhere. And so the three went on quarreling until a cry and then another was heard coming from the stable. They looked up.

"What's the matter?" asked Wrangel, but now all was quiet. "Who screamed out there?" asked Wrangel. "What is going on out there?"

"Oh, sir!" said the innkeeper.

"What is it?" Wrangel cried. "What's the matter?"

"Just imagine, sire," said the innkeeper, "the young wife gave birth to a child, a boy. Perhaps, after all, peace will come soon."

The three looked at one another. For a long time they had not heard anyone speak in tones such as the innkeeper used. The child was the child of strangers, it was no concern of his, and yet he was as moved as if it had indeed been his own. For here, in this destroyed countryside, resembling an icy waste covered with the corpses of the dead, a child had begun to live—breathing a breath of spring. In the midst of the triumph of death, which was the daily business of the generals, a child had been born, and it seemed as if it had been born also unto them.

The first to step through the threshold of the stable door was Melander. He was followed by Wrangel, and then Turenne. There lay the woman on her bed of straw. The others knelt around her as they wrapped the baby in a few odds and ends of old rags and laid the child in her arms.

The generals stood there in silence and gazed upon the mother and child for a long time. Then Turenne removed the golden chain which he wore under his Twelfth Night robe and placed it near the child. Melander pulled off his glove and took a ruby ring from his finger, and Wrangel laid a pouch full of money down on the bed of straw.

To those who received the gifts, it seemed as if a miracle had happened. The young man wanted to express his faltering thanks but was not able to utter a single word. They soon departed, leaving behind them their strange lantern, and ordered the innkeeper, who was chattering and laughing and who continued to wipe his eyes, to stay behind when he wanted to accompany them.

At the outskirts of the village, they saluted one another curtly, and each one went on his way, their talk unfinished.

But in their hearts was peace.

Gifts from the Heart

THE ART OF GIVING

Gerald Horton Bath

One of my favorite stories is about a missionary teaching in Africa. Before Christmas, he had been telling his African students how Christians, as an expression of their joy, gave each other presents on Christ's birthday.

On Christmas morning one of the Africans brought the missionary a seashell of lustrous beauty. When asked where he had discovered such an extraordinary shell, the young man said he had walked many miles to a certain bay, the only spot where such shells could be found.

"I think it was wonderful of you to travel so far to get this lovely gift for me," the teacher exclaimed.

His eyes brightening, the African answered, "Long walk, part of gift."

A gift, however small, speaks its own language. And when it tells of the love of the giver, it is truly blessed.
—*Norman Vincent Peale*

CHRISTMAS IS IN THE UNEXPECTED

Faith Baldwin

Christmas is in the unexpected gift: flowers from an acquaintance; a telephone call from someone you haven't heard from in years, and who, you thought, had forgotten you; it is in a card from overseas, a letter from a stranger, and a clumsily wrapped, handmade atrocity, fashioned by a child who has labored long, and with sticky hands.

None of this is basically material.

Christmas is an urge to give, to do, to be. It may last a very short time— and usually does—but, during it, the human spirit attains a fractional growth.

A Gift from the Heart

Norman Vincent Peale

New York City, where I live, is impressive at any time, but as Christmas approaches, it's overwhelming. Store windows blaze—with light and color, furs and jewels. Golden angels, forty feet tall, hover over Fifth Avenue. Wealth, power, opulence . . . nothing in the world can match this fabulous display.

Through the gleaming canyons, people hurry to find last-minute gifts. Money seems to be no problem. If there's a problem, it's that the recipients so often have everything they need or want that it's hard to find anything suitable, anything that will really say "I love you."

Last December, as Christ's birthday drew near, a stranger was faced with just that problem. She had come from Switzerland to live in an American home and perfect her English. In return, she was willing to act as secretary, mind the grandchildren, do anything she was asked. She was just a girl in her late teens. Her name was Ursula.

One of the tasks her employers gave Ursula was keeping track of Christmas presents as they arrived. There were many, and all would require an acknowledgement. Ursula kept a faithful record but with a growing sense of concern. She was grateful to her American friends; she wanted to show her gratitude by giving them a Christmas present. But nothing that she could buy with her small allowance could compare with the gifts she was recording daily. Besides, even without these gifts, it seemed to her that her employer already had everything.

At night, from her window, Ursula could see the snowy expanse of Central Park and beyond it the jagged skyline of the city. Far below, in the restless streets, taxis hooted and traffic lights winked red and green. It was so different from the silent majesty of the Alps that at times she had to blink back tears of the homesickness she was careful never to show. It was in the solitude of her little room, a few days before Christmas, that her secret idea came to Ursula.

It was almost as if a voice spoke clearly, inside her head. "It's true," said the voice, "that many people in this city have much more than you do. But surely there are many people who have far less. If thou will think about this, you may find a solution to what's troubling you."

Ursula thought long and hard. Finally on her day off, which was Christmas Eve, she went to a great department store. She moved slowly along the crowded aisles, selecting and rejecting things in her mind. At last she bought something, and had it wrapped in gaily colored paper. She went out into the gray twilight and looked helplessly around. Finally she went up to a doorman, resplendent in blue and gold. "Excuse, please," she said in her hesitant English, "can you tell me where to find a poor street?"

"A poor street, miss?" said the puzzled man.

"Yes, a very poor street. The poorest in the city."

The doorman looked doubtful. "Well, you might try Harlem. Or down in the Village. Or the Lower East Side, maybe."

But these names meant nothing to Ursula. She thanked the doorman and walked along, threading her way through the stream of shoppers until she came to a tall policeman. "Please," she said, "can you direct me to a very poor street in . . . in Harlem?"

The policeman looked at her sharply and shook his head. "Harlem's no place for you, miss." And he blew his whistle and sent the traffic swirling past.

Holding her package carefully, Ursula walked on, head bowed against the sharp wind. If a street looked poorer than the one she was on, she took it. But none seemed like the slums she had heard about. Once she stopped a woman, "Please, where do the very poor people live?" But the woman gave her a stare and hurried on.

Darkness came sifting from the sky, Ursula was cold and discouraged and afraid of becoming lost. She came to an intersection and stood forlornly on the corner. What she was trying to do suddenly seemed foolish, impulsive, absurd. Then, through the traffic's roar, she heard the cheerful tinkle of a bell. On the corner opposite, a Salvation Army man was making his traditional Christmas appeal.

At once Ursula felt better; the Salvation Army was a part of life in Switzerland, too. Surely this man could tell her what she wanted to know. She waited for the light, then crossed over to him. "Can you help me? I'm looking for a baby. I have here a little present for the poorest baby I can find." And she held up the package with the green ribbon and the gaily colored paper.

Dressed in gloves and overcoat a size too big for him, he seemed a very ordinary man. But behind his steel-rimmed glasses his eyes were kind. He looked at Ursula and stopped ringing his bell. "What sort of present?" he asked.

"A little dress. For a small, poor baby. Do you know of one?"

"Oh, yes," he said. "'Of more than one, I'm afraid."

"Is it far away? I could take a taxi, maybe?"

The Salvation Army man wrinkled his forehead. Finally he said, "It's almost six o'clock. My relief will show up then. If you want to wait, and if you afford a dollar taxi ride, I'll take you to a family in my neighborhood who needs just about everything."

"And they have a small baby?"

"A very small baby."

"Then," said Ursula joyfully, "I wait!"

The substitute bell-ringer came. A cruising taxi slowed. In its welcome warmth, she told her new friend about herself, how she came to be in New York, what she was trying to do. He listened in silence, and the taxi driver listened too. When they reached their destination, the driver said, "Take your time, missy, I'll wait for you."

On the sidewalk, Ursula stared up at the forbidding tenement—dark, decaying, saturated with hopelessness. A gust of wind, iron-cold, stirred the refuse in the street and rattled the reeling trash cans. "They live on the third floor," the Salvation Army man said. "Shall we go up?"

But Ursula shook her head. "They would try to thank me, and this is not from me." She pressed the package into his hand. "Take it up for me, please. Say it's from . . . from someone who has everything."

The taxi bore her swiftly from dark streets to lighted ones, from misery to abundance. She tried to visualize the Salvation Army man climbing the stairs, the knock, the explanation, the package being opened, the dress on the baby. It was hard to do.

Arriving at the apartment house on Fifth Avenue where she lived, she fumbled in her purse. But the driver flicked the flag up. "No charge, miss."

"No charge?" echoed Ursula, bewildered.

"Don't worry," the driver said. "I've been paid." He smiled at her and drove away.

Ursula was up early the next day. She set the table with special care. By the time she had finished, the family was awake, and there was all the excitement and laughter of Christmas morning. Soon the living room was a sea of gay discarded wrappings. Ursula thanked everyone for the presents she received. Finally when there was a lull, she began to explain hesitantly why there

seemed to be none from her. She told about going to the department store. She told about the Salvation Army man. She told about the taxi driver. When she finished, there was a long silence. No one seemed to trust himself to speak. "So you see," said Ursula, "I try to do a kindness in your name. And this is my Christmas present to you."

How do I happen to know all this? I know it because ours was the home where Ursula lived. Ours was the Christmas she shared. We were like many Americans, so richly blessed that to this child from across the sea there seemed to be nothing she could add to the material things we already had. And so she offered something of far greater value: a gift from the heart, an act of kindness carried out in our name.

Strange, isn't it? A shy Swiss girl, alone in a great impersonal city. You would think that nothing she could do would affect anyone. And yet, by trying to give away love, she brought the true spirit of Christmas into our lives, the spirit of selfless giving. That was Ursula's secret—and she shared it with us all.

The Heart Goes Home

Grace V. Watkins

Always the heart goes home on Christmas Eve,
Goes silently across a continent,
Or mountains, or the seas. A heart will leave
The glitter of a city street and, sent
By something deep and timeless, find the way
To a little cottage on a country hill.
And even if the little cottage may
Have disappeared, a heart will find it still.

The smile of tenderness upon the faces,
The simple words, the arms secure and strong,
The sweetness of the well-remembered places;
All these a heart will find and will belong
Once more to country hills, however far,
And sense the holy presence of the Star.

Lord of All
Robert Herrick

The darling of the world is come,
And fit it is, we find a room
To welcome Him, to welcome Him.
The nobler part of all the house here
    is the heart,
Which we will give Him;
And bequeath this holly
    and this ivy wreath
To do Him honour; who's our King,
And Lord of all this revelling.

Little Things Remembered
Alice Leedy Mason

The heart goes home at Christmas across the miles and years;
Amid the splendor of the day the memory appears.
Silver bells ring out again with gladness in their chimes,
But never quite as rich and clear as those remembered times.
The carolers have made their rounds to hail this blessed night.
The heart hears other voices ring with Yule logs burning bright.
Christmas candles everywhere send out a special glow—
These burning tapers bring to light sweet scenes of long ago.
The beauty of the Eastern star is marvelous to behold—
A changeless fact in times of change, so new, and yet so old.
The church in all its splendor is waiting hushed and still,
But memory seeks a smaller church and climbs a starlit hill.
The star . . . the bells . . . the music . . . are treasures set apart.
These little things remembered keep Christmas in the heart.

When Christmastime makes its approach, my heart is homeward bound. —Virginia Blanck Moore

Joy to the World

Isaac Watts

George F. Handel

1. Joy to the world, the Lord is come! Let earth re-
2. Joy to the earth, the Sav - iour reigns! Let men their
3. No more let sin and sor - row grow, nor thorns in -
4. He rules the world with truth and grace, and makes the

ceive her King; let ev - 'ry heart pre-
songs em - ploy; while fields and floods, rocks,
fest the ground; He comes to make His
na - tions prove the glo - ries of His

WHAT SHALL WE DO THIS CHRISTMAS?

Colleen Townsend Evans

We were in Scotland, my husband and I, and away from home at Christmastime for the first time in our lives. It was December 1953. We had been married three years and Louie was studying at the University of Edinburgh. Our first child, Danny, had been born two months ago—just a few weeks after we arrived in Scotland—and he made us a family—but such a small one!

My husband and I were accustomed to large family gatherings at Christmas and we were beginning to feel the loneliness that comes to those who are among unfamiliar faces and surroundings at a time of the year when the familiar is deeply recalled—and needed. It wouldn't be the same for us this year. Much as we loved Scotland and were warmed by the people we met, they weren't "family" in the traditional sense.

Before we were married we each spent the holidays at home among friends and relatives who came to be with us. Louie's family was large and mine was small, but our numbers always swelled at Christmas. And during the days before Christmas, we knew the excitement of the familiar preparations—choosing the tree, unwrapping the ornaments, remembering the words to the lovely carols, the warm embrace of friends, the sudden, unguarded smiles from strangers passing on the street or in the stores, baking the pies for Christmas dinner, wrapping the presents. . . . These were our traditions. These were the things we always did. This was the way Christmas always was for us . . . and these customs gave us a secure, comfortable feeling of being able to hold onto the familiar in a world that was always new and different.

After we were married, we spent Christmas day with my parents, and Louie's parents went to the home of one of his sisters. But still the traditions were kept intact and the familiar, lovable faces were there . . . and it was fun, fun, fun!

"What shall we do at Christmas this year?" we asked ourselves as we began to feel the first pangs of hunger for our families. No answer.

In Scotland we were foreign students, and as such we were invited to an international student party where we met some delightful young men and

women from many different countries. They too were away from home and familiar faces. We felt especially drawn to two students from Nigeria—Sam and his beautiful cousin Iba. In the days following the party we saw quite a lot of them and got to know them very well. And then, one day when the question, "What shall we do at Christmas?" came up, the answer was obvious. Invite Sam and Iba to spend the day with us! Just because we weren't back home in the familiar surroundings, keeping the old traditions, sharing the day with our family-family, that didn't mean we had to be alone. Right outside our door there was another family that extended throughout the whole world . . . there were people who needed to be included in our lives just as much as we needed to have them with us. Sam and Iba—and any of their friends who didn't have a place to go on Christmas day—they were our heart-family!

On the other three Christmases we had spent as a married couple, my parents were the ones who did everything for me. They prepared the dinner and opened their house to us . . . and during all the other earlier years of my life I had been poured into by those who loved and cared for me. . . . I had been the child receiving, but now it was different . . . I was the woman whose privilege it was to provide, to prepare. I loved the feeling of it!

And prepare I did. I wanted to blend as many of our cultural traditions into the newness of our situation as I possibly could. We had a tree—a small one—decorated with a few ornaments I bought at the five-and-ten. Louie supplied the wood for our fireplace and we had a crackling fire burning all day, which thoroughly delighted our little son. I tried to collect the ingredients for a typical American Christmas dinner, but since some items were scarce (the war was not long over) I had to improvise. For instance, I couldn't get sweet potatoes, so I cooked carrots in large chunks and baked them with brown sugar.

We spent Christmas day in 1953 with our heart-family—Sam and Iba and a room full of other students who came in their colorful native dress. It was a wonderful day, one I shall never forget. We read the Christmas story from Matthew and Luke and we sang carols and laughed and embraced and shared the deep joy we felt in the knowledge that we were children of God. The Nigerians were such lively, animated people who spoke so openly of their love for Christ . . . and it was this love which bound us together, making us truly brothers and sisters of one another. And then I understood what Jesus meant when he said, "Who is my brother and my sister? These people are, those who do the will of God." Sam and Iba and their wonderful friends were our friends now . . . they were new to my life . . . they were not part of my past . . . they were not the familiar faces I had longed to see at Christmas—but they were part of my present and part of my future. And they were our family!

Because we were unable to keep our traditional Christmas that year, we spent it in untraditional ways . . . and we discovered that it is more important to keep the spirit of Christmas than to keep the customs with which we have grown up. Yes, we still love the traditions and keep them whenever we can, and we love to be with our family-family whenever we can . . . but we are grateful for the times when this was not possible, for the times when we couldn't be with our relatives and friends—and yet Christmas still happened . . . and in a most spirit-warming way.

Sometimes life doesn't come to us; sometimes we have to reach out for it. People won't always come to us and instead of sitting home, waiting for someone to arrive, succumbing to the loneliness that comes to all of us when we are not with those who care for us, we have to reach out to those we need. Instead of asking ourselves, "Who's going to invite me for dinner?" why not ask, "Whom can I cook dinner for?"

After we returned from Scotland we began to form our own Christmas traditions as a family. Instead of going to my parents, we had them with us in our home, first in Bel Air and then in La Jolla, California, where Louie was called to serve two wonderful churches. As our children grew up they looked forward to these special gatherings each year. There were six of us now in our nuclear family—Louie and I, and our four children, Dan, Tim, Andie, and Jim—and at Christmastime our house was filled with friends as well as relatives and that was the only place in the world where we wanted to be on that day.

A few years ago my husband received a call to National Presbyterian Church in Washington, D.C., and we knew that that year would be our last in La Jolla. Our family gathering would be especially dear to us, for we would carry its memories for a long, long time.

And then we learned that my parents—Grandma and Grandpa Wilhelm—would not be with us. Grandpa had to undergo surgery and would have to spend Christmas day in a hospital north of Los Angeles. So we mailed our gifts to each other and bit our lips a little in our disappointment.

If it had been just Louie and I at Christmas, I would have suggested driving up to Los Angeles and spending the day with Grandpa, but I just couldn't

ask our children to do that. The trip took three-and-a-half hours each way, which meant that we would have to be away from home all day, and our sons and daughter so enjoyed being home at Christmas. I knew their friends would be dropping in all day—and that soon our children would be saying good-bye to these friends for at least a long time. So I put the idea out of my mind.

On Christmas morning we did what we always did as a family. We got up very early, had a light breakfast and then we sat around the tree while one of us read the Christmas story from the Gospels. Then we opened our presents, hugging and kissing each other for the thoughtfulness and remembered wishes we found wrapped up in the packages. But it wasn't the same without Grandma and Grandpa. We missed them very much. Our tall, long-haired boys were touchingly open about their feelings. "I sure miss Grandpa." "He's so much fun!" "Yea, he's a real cruiser!" and Andie's sensitive face and the sadness in her large compassionate eyes said more than words.

It was time for me to take the turkey out of the refrigerator and put it in the oven, and I was glad to have an excuse to go into the kitchen because I thought I was going to cry a little. And I honestly don't know which one of our children said it first, but somebody said, "Hey, how would the rest of you

feel about driving up to Los Angeles and seeing Grandma and Grandpa?"

Before I reached the kitchen the others agreed.

"Yeah, that's what I'd like to do!"

"Let's drive up and see them."

"It's not the same without them."

The turkey never got out of the refrigerator that Christmas day. We left it, stuffed and ready, for another time. We piled into the car. We took along our projector and a few slides from our summer backpacking trip so that we could show them to my parents.

It was a long drive to the hospital and when we got there the corridors were almost empty. Doctors had sent home as many patients as they could, because everyone knows that a hospital is no place to spend the holidays. We found Grandpa's room and looked in. There he was, sitting up in bed, with Grandma in a straight-backed chair by his bedside. When Grandpa saw us, the tears began to roll down his cheeks and he cried like a little boy overwhelmed with a joy that is just too big for him to hold inside himself. He couldn't get over the fact that we—and especially the children—would choose to drive so far to be with him on this day, this year.

We had a wonderful visit and Grandpa kept saying, "This is the best Christmas I've ever had." We talked and laughed and showed our slides on the white hospital walls and reminisced about our summer vacation in the Sierras. We stayed for several hours, and before we left we all joined hands around Grandpa's bed and thanked God for this day when we were able to be together with our loved ones.

When we left Grandpa's room, we were hungry so we went downstairs to the hospital cafeteria which was about to close. There was very little food left—some cole slaw, some dishes of gelatin with whipped cream, and a few cartons of milk—and that was our Christmas dinner. I'm sure that everyone felt as I did, that it was one of the richest Christmases we'd ever had.

On the way home we were cozy and close in our car and so filled with the spirit of Christmas. Once again life had shown us that traditions, lovely as they are, do not make Christmas. Christmas happens wherever we are—at home, in another land, among friends and family, among strangers, in a hospital room, on the road to somewhere—in the midst of the familiar or on the threshold of the new and unexpected—as long as our hearts are open to the love that Christ brought us when Christmas happened that first time.

A Prayer at Christmas

Author Unknown

Give us the faith of innocent children, that we may look forward with hope in our hearts to the dawn of happy tomorrows. Reawaken the thought that our most cherished desires will be realized—the things closest to our hearts—that we may come to an appreciation of the limitless joys and bountiful rewards of Patience, Charity, and Sacrifice.

Above all, endow us with the spirit of courage, that we may face the perplexities of a troubled world without flinching, imbued with the child-like faith which envisions the beautiful and inspiring things of life, and restore the happy hours and experiences so many of us foolishly believe are lost forever.

Give us faith in ourselves and faith in our fellow man, then the treasures and beauties of life that make man happy will spring from an inexhaustible source.

And at Christmas, when the hearts of the world swell in joyous celebration, let us cast aside the pretense of sturdy men and live, if only for a day, in the hope and joy we knew as children.

A Prayer for Christmas Morning

Henry Van Dyke

The day of joy returns, Father in Heaven, and crowns another year with peace and good will. Help us rightly to remember the birth of Jesus, that we may share in the song of the angels, the gladness of the shepherds, and the worship of the wise men. Close the doors of hate and open the doors of love all over the world. . . . Let kindness come with every gift and good desires with every greeting. Deliver us from evil, by the blessing that Christ brings, and teach us to be merry with clean hearts. May the Christmas morning make us happy to be thy children, and the Christmas evening bring us to our bed with grateful thoughts, forgiving and forgiven, for Jesus' sake. Amen.

THE YEAR THE PRESENTS DIDN'T COME

Ben Logan

Catalogs, it must be understood, were our department stores. Visitors from a marvelous place somewhere outside our world, they said Christmas was coming, that once a year a spirit of extravagance brought us a select few of all the wonderful things on display.

The catalog orders would go into the mail and our choices began to grow, becoming our own creations. Every morning when I first woke up, I would stay under the covers a moment, shut my eyes tight and try to see what was happening. After five days, I decided the letter had arrived in Chicago. Two more days—no, make it three because they were busy—to find our things and ship them. Then another five days for the packages to come. I added one more day because that made it Saturday and I could run to meet the mailman myself. Mr. Holliday was driving a sled by then because there was too much snow for his Model T. He poked through the packages in the sled box. "Sorry," he said. "Not here yet."

The days crept by. Each afternoon we waited in the cold for Mr. Holliday. He would search through the sled for the packages he already knew were not there and say, "Maybe tomorrow."

On the day before Christmas, we raced to the mailbox with a pail of steaming coffee for Mr. Holliday. "You know," he said, not looking at us, "I guess nothing came, but I'll just look one more time." He sorted through the packages. We knew there wasn't anything there for us. He was just trying to make us feel better, or maybe make himself feel better.

We stayed there at the mailbox looking at each other. We didn't believe it. I was crying when we went to the house. Mother held me. "We'll still have Christmas, you know."

"Without our presents?"

Something changed in her face. "There's more to Christmas than presents."

When we carried the tree in and set it up in the dining room, the fresh snow began to melt into hundreds of shiny beads of water.

"Look!" Mother said. "It's already decorated."

We popped corn and made strings, the white corn alternating with the

cranberries. We got out all the old ornaments, handing to Father the star that went beyond our reach. The folded paper ornaments were opened to become bright-colored balls, stars, and bells. Mother began to hum a Christmas carol. It was just like all the other remembered afternoons leading up to Christmas Eve.

The house was very still when I woke on Christmas morning. Treelike patterns of frost covered the lower half of my window, turned red-gold by the beginning color on the eastern horizon. Far out across a white meadow I could see smoke rising from the chimney of a neighbor's house, reminding me that other people were having Christmas.

For each of us there was a basket filled with English walnuts, pecans, almonds, ribbon candy, peanut brittle, chocolate stars, and one bright navel orange and a big Red Delicious apple. I sorted through my basket, silenced by the strangeness of having no presents to open and the thought of an empty day stretching ahead.

Mother went to the kitchen to work on Christmas dinner. We four boys followed and worked with her. I don't think that had ever happened before. My new toys had always captured me on Christmas morning, pulling me away into a play world that did not include anyone else.

We made sugar cookies, eating them hot and buttery right from the oven almost as fast as we cut out new ones. The chickens were already cooking, filling the house with a rich roasting smell. Junior brought his guitar into the kitchen and we sang as we worked. Not Christmas carols. They were for later. Everyone kept talking about earlier Christmases, every other sentence beginning with "Remember the time . . ."

Everyone was busy every minute. There were hickory nuts to crack, bowls to lick, coffee to grind, cream to whip. We kept splitting more firewood and feeding the kitchen range to keep the fire just right.

Finally, we all helped carry the steaming dishes to the dining room table with its white tablecloth that was trimmed with lace. There was a solemn moment and then the food itself, delicious and unending.

After dinner, Father left the table and put on his heavy jacket. We knew what he was going to do. Every year he took down a sheaf of oats that had been hanging on the wall since harvest and carried it outside for the birds. This time we put on our coats and went with him.

"It was something we did in Norway," he told us. "But there it would always be wheat."

He hung the oats on the big maple tree and we stepped back and waited, standing very still. A blue jay swooped in and peered at the grain. A bright red cardinal came and began to eat. Then a whole flock of English sparrows arrived, noisy and quarrelsome, reminding me of the four of us.

We cleared the snow away, brought kindling and sticks of oak from the woodshed and soon had a roaring bonfire in the yard. I ran to tell Mother, and she put on her coat and joined us.

Even then I don't think I realized how different the day had been. That is the way of Christmas stories. Their meanings have to grow with the seasons and the telling, and we only remember what we have learned by keeping the past alive.

Gifts *from* On High

THE SPIRIT OF GIVING

Kate Douglas Wiggin

When the Child of Nazareth was born, the sun, according to the Bosnian legend, "leaped in the heavens, and the stars around it danced. A peace came over mountain and forest. Even the rotten stump stood straight and healthy on the green hillside. The grass was beflowered with open blossoms, incense sweet as myrrh pervaded upland and forest, birds sang on the mountain top, and all gave thanks to the great God."

It is naught but an old folktale, but it has truth hidden at its heart, for a strange, subtle force, a spirit of genial goodwill, a newborn kindness, seem to animate child and man alike when the world pays its tribute to the "heaven-sent youngling," as the poet Drummond calls the infant Christ.

When the three wise men rode from the east into the west on that "first, best Christmas night," they bore on their saddlebows three caskets filled with gold and frankincense and myrrh to be laid at the feet of the manger-cradled babe of Bethlehem. Beginning with this old, old journey, the spirit of giving crept into the world's heart. As the Magi came bearing gifts, so do we also; gifts that relieve wants, gifts that are sweet and fragrant with friendship, gifts that breathe love, gifts that mean service, gifts inspired still by the star that shone over the city of David nearly two thousand years ago.

Then hang the green coronet of the Christmas-tree with glittering baubles and jewels of flame; heap offerings on its emerald branches; bring the Yule log to the firing; deck the house with holly and mistletoe,

And all the bells on earth shall ring
On Christmas day in the morning.

Who can forget—never to be forgot—the time, that all the world in slumber lies, when, like the stars, the singing angels shot to earth, and heaven awaked all his eyes to see another sun at midnight rise. —Giles Fletcher

Christmas Carol

J. R. Newell

From the starry heaven's descending
Herald angels in their flight,
Nearer winging,
Clearer singing,
Thrilled with harmony the night:
"Glory, glory in the highest!"
Sounded yet and yet again,
Sweeter, clearer,
Fuller, nearer–
"Peace on earth, good will to men!"

Shepherds in the field abiding,
Roused from sleep, that gladsome morn,
Saw the glory,
Heard the story
That the Prince of Peace was born:
"Glory, glory in the highest!"
Sang the angel choir again,
Nearer winging,
Clearer singing:
"Peace on earth, good will to men!"

Swept the angel singers onward,
Died the song upon the air;
But the glory
Of that story
Grows and triumphs everywhere.
And when glow the Yuletide heavens,
Seems that glorious song again
Floating nearer,
Sweeter, clearer–
"Peace on earth, good will to men!"

Rise up, Shepherd, and Follow

Author Unknown

There's a star in the East
On Christmas morn.
Rise up, shepherd, and follow!
It'll lead to the place
Where the Saviour's born.
Rise up, shepherd, and follow!
If you take good heed
To the angel's words and
Rise up, shepherd, and follow,
You'll forget your flocks,
You'll forget your herds.
Rise up, shepherd, and follow!
Leave your sheep, leave your lambs,
Rise up, shepherd, and follow!
Leave your ewes, leave your rams,
Rise up, shepherd, and follow!
Follow the Star of Bethlehem,
Rise up, shepherd, and follow!

There's a song in the air!
There's a star in the sky!
There's a mother's deep
prayer and a baby's low
cry! —Josiah Gilbert Holland

CHRISTMAS ROSES

Alice Isabel Hazeltine

The sun had dropped below the western hills of Judea, and the stillness of night had covered the earth. The heavens were illumined only by numberless stars, which shone the brighter for the darkness of the sky. No sound was heard but the occasional howl of a jackal or the bleat of a lamb in the sheepfold. Inside a tent on the hillside slept the shepherd, Berachah, and his daughter, Madelon. The little girl lay restless—sleeping, waking, dreaming, until at last she roused herself and looked about her.

"Father," she whispered, "Oh, my father, awake. I fear for the sheep."

The shepherd turned himself and reached for his staff. "What hearest thou, daughter? The dogs are asleep. Hast thou been burdened by an evil dream?"

"Nay, but Father," she answered, "seest thou not the light? Hearest thou not the voice?"

Berachah gathered his mantle about him, rose, looked over the hills toward Bethlehem, and listened. The olive trees on yonder slope were casting their shadows in a marvellous light, unlike daybreak or sunset, or even the light of the moon. By the campfire below on the hillside the shepherds on watch were rousing themselves. Berachah waited and wondered, while Madelon clung to his side. Suddenly a sound rang out in the stillness. Madelon pressed still closer.

"It is the voice of an angel, my daughter. What it means I know not. Neither understand I this light." Berachah fell on his knees and prayed.

"Fear not: for, behold, I bring you good tidings of great joy, which shall be to all people. For unto you is born this day in the city of David a Saviour, which is Christ the Lord. And this shall be a sign unto you; Ye shall find the babe wrapped in swaddling clothes, lying in a manger."

The voice of the angel died away, and the air was filled with music. Berachah raised Madelon to her feet. "Ah, daughter," said he, "it is the wonder night so long expected. To us hath it been given to see the sign. It is the Messiah who hath come, the Messiah, whose name shall be called Wonderful, Counsellor, the mighty God, the Everlasting Father, the Prince of Peace. He it is who shall reign on the throne of David, He it is who shall redeem Israel."

Slowly up the hillside toiled the shepherds to the tent of Berachah, their chief, who rose to greet them eagerly.

"What think you of the wonder night and of the sign?" he queried. "Are we not above all others honored, to learn of the Messiah's coming?"

"Yea, and Berachah," replied their spokesman, Simon, "believest thou not that we should worship the infant King? Let us now go to Bethlehem and see this thing which has come to pass."

A murmur of protest came from the edge of the circle, and one or two turned impatiently away, whispering of duty toward flocks and the folly of searching for a new-born baby in the city of Bethlehem. Hardheaded, practical men were these, whose hearts had not been touched by vision or by song.

The others, however, turned expectantly toward Berachah, awaiting his decision. "Truly," said Jude, "the angel of the Lord hath given us the sign in order that we might go to worship Him. How can we then do otherwise? We shall find Him, as we have heard, lying in a manger. Let us not tarry, but let us gather our choicest treasures to lay at His feet and set out without delay across the hills toward Bethlehem."

"Oh, my Father," whispered Madelon, "permit me to go with thee." Berachah did not hear her but bade the men gather together their gifts.

"I, too, father?" asked Madelon. Still Berachah said nothing. Madelon slipped back into the tent, and throwing her arms around Melampo, her shepherd dog, whispered in his ear.

Soon the shepherds returned with their gifts. Simple treasures they were— a pair of cloves, a fine wool blanket, some eggs, some honey, some late autumn fruits. Berachah had searched for the finest of his flock—a snow-white lamb. Across the hills toward Bethlehem in the quiet, star-lit night they journeyed. As they moved silently along, the snow beneath their feet was changed to grass and flowers, and the icicles which had dropped from the trees covered their pathway like stars in the Milky Way.

Following at a distance, yet close enough to see them, came Madelon with Melampo at her heels. Over the hills they travelled on until Madelon lost sight of their own hillside. Farther and farther the shepherds went until they passed David's well and entered the city. Berachah led the way.

"How shall we know?" whispered Simon. And the others answered, "Hush, we must await the sign."

When at last they had compassed the crescent of Bethlehem's hills, they halted by an open doorway at a signal from their leader. "The manger," they joyfully murmured, "the manger! We have found the new-born King!"

One by one the shepherds entered. One by one they fell on their knees. Away in the shadow stood the little girl, her hand on Melampo's head. In wonder she gazed while the shepherds presented their gifts and were permitted each to hold for a moment the newborn Saviour. Melampo, the shepherd dog, crouched on the ground, as if he too, like the ox and the ass within, would worship the Child. Madelon turned toward the darkness weeping. Then, lifting her face to heaven, she prayed that God would bless Mother and Baby. Melampo moved closer to her, dumbly offering his companionship, and, raising his head, seemed to join in her petition. Once more she looked at the worshipping circle.

"Alas," she grieved, "no gift have I for the infant Saviour. Would that I had but a flower to place in His hand."

Suddenly Melampo stirred by her side, and as she turned again from the manger she saw before her an angel, the light from whose face illumined the darkness and whose look of tenderness rested on her tear-stained eyes.

"Why grievest thou, maiden?" asked the angel.

"That I come empty-handed to the cradle of the Saviour, that I bring no gift to greet Him," she murmured.

"The gift of thine heart, that is the best of all," answered the angel. "But that thou mayst carry something to the manger, see, I will strike with my staff upon the ground."

Wonderingly Madelon waited. From the dry earth wherever the angel's staff had touched sprang fair, white roses. Timidly she stretched out her hand toward the nearest ones. In the light of the angel's smile she gathered them, until her arms were filled with flowers. Again she turned toward the manger and quietly slipped to the circle of kneeling shepherds.

Closer she crept to the Child, longing, yet fearing, to offer her gift.

"How shall I know," she pondered, "whether He will receive this my gift as His own?

Berachah gazed in amazement at Madelon and the roses which she held. How came his child there, his child whom he had left safe on the hillside? And whence came such flowers? Truly this was a wonder night.

Step by step she neared the manger, knelt, and placed a rose in the Baby's hand. As the shepherds watched in silence, Mary bent over her Child, and Madelon waited for a sign. "Will He accept them?" she questioned. "How, oh, how shall I know?" As she prayed in humble silence, the Baby's eyes opened slowly, and over His face spread a smile.

Christmas Still

Phillips Brooks

The silent skies are full of speech
For who hath ears to hear;
The winds are whispering each to each,
The moon is calling to the beech,
And stars their sacred mission teach,
Of Faith and Love and Fear.

But once the sky its silence broke
And song o'erflowed the earth,
The midnight air with glory shook,
And angels mortal language spoke
When God our human nature took
In Christ the Savior's birth.

And Christmas once is Christmas still;
The gates through which He came,
And forests wild and murmuring rill,
And fruitful field and breezy hill,
And all that else the wide world fill
Are vocal with His name.

The sky can still remember it,
The earliest Christmas morn,
When in the cold December
The Savior Christ was born;
And still in darkness clouded
And still in noonday light,
It feels its far depths crowded
With Angels fair and bright.

No star unfolds its glory,
No trumpet's wind is blown,
But tells the Christmas story
In music of its own.
No eager strife of mortals,
In busy fields or town,
But sees the open portals
Through which the Christ came down.

Angels We Have Heard on High

TRADITIONAL FRENCH

1. An - gels we have heard on high, Sweet - ly sing - ing o'er the plains;
2. Shep-herds, why this ju - bi-lee? Why your joy - ous strains pro-long?
3. Come to Beth - le - hem, and see Him whose birth the an - gels sing;
4. See Him in a man - ger laid, Whom the choirs of an - gels praise;

And the moun-tains in re-ply, Ech - o back their joy - ous strains.
What the glad-some tid - ings be Which in - spire your heav'n - ly song?
Come, a - dore on bend - ed knee Christ the Lord, the new-born King.
Ma - ry, Jo - seph, lend your aid, While our hearts in love we raise.

Christmas

Faith Baldwin

The snow is full of silver light
Spilled from the heavens' tilted cup,
And on this holy, tranquil night,
The eyes of men are lifted up
To see the promise written fair,
The hope of peace for all on earth,

And hear the singing bells declare
The marvel of the dear Christ's birth.
The way from year to year is long
And though the road be dark so far,
Bright is the manger, sweet the song;
The steeple rises to the Star.

What Means This Glory Round Our Feet?

James Russell Lowell

"What means this glory round our feet,"
The magi mused, "more bright than morn?"
And voices chanted clear and sweet,
"Today the Prince of Peace is born."

"What means that star," the shepherds said,
"That brightens through the rocky glen?"
And angels, answering overhead,
Sang, "Peace on earth, good will to men."

All round about our feet shall shine
A Light like that the wise men saw,

If we our loving wills incline
To that sweet life which is the law.

So shall we learn to understand
The simple faith of shepherds then,
And clasping kindly hand in hand,
Sing, "Peace on earth, good will to men."

And they who to their childhood cling
And keep at eve the faith of morn,
Shall daily hear the angels sing,
"Today the Prince of Peace is born."

O star of wonder, star of night, Star with royal beauty bright, Westward leading, still proceeding, Guide us to thy perfect light. —John Henry Hopkins Jr.

The Sending of the Magi

Bliss Carman

In a far Eastern country it happened long of yore,
Where a lone and level sunrise flushes the desert floor,
That three kings sat together and a spearman kept the door.
Gaspar, whose wealth was counted by city and caravan;
With Melchior, the seer who read the starry plan;
And Balthasar, the blameless, who loved his fellow man.

There while they talked, a sudden strange rushing sound arose,
And as with startled faces they thought upon their foes,
Three figures stood before them in imperial repose.
One in flame-gold and one in blue and one in scarlet clear,
With the almighty portent of sunrise they drew near!
And the kings made obeisance with hand on breast, in fear.

"Arise," said they, "we bring you good tidings of great peace!
Today a power is wakened whose working must increase
Till fear and greed and malice and violence shall cease."
The messengers were Michael, by whom all things were wrought
To shape and hue; and Gabriel who is the lord of thought;
And Rafael without whose love all toil must come to nought.

Then while the kings' hearts greatened and all the chamber shone,
As when the hills at sundown take a new glory on
And the air thrills with purple, their visitors were gone.
Then straightway up rose Gaspar, Melchior, and Balthasar
And passed out through the murmur of palace and bazaar
To make without misgiving the journey of the Star.

The Ballad of Befana

Phyllis McGinley

Befana, the housewife, scrubbing her pane,
Saw three old sages ride down the lane,
Saw three gray travelers pass her door—
Gaspar, Balthazar, and Melchior.
"Where journey you, Sirs?" she asked of them.
And Gaspar answered, "To Bethlehem,
For we have news of a marvelous thing:
Born in a stable is Christ the King."

"Give Him my welcome!" Balthazar smiled,
"Come with us, Mistress, to greet the Child."
"Oh, happily, happily would I fare
Were my dusting through and I'd polished the stair."
Old Melchior leaned on his saddle horn.
"Then send but a gift to the small newborn."
"Oh, gladly, gladly I'd send Him one
Were my cupboards clean and my weaving done.
I'd give Him a robe to warm His sleep,
But first I must mend the fire and sweep.
As soon as ever I've baked my bread,
I'll fetch Him a pillow for His head
And a coverlet too," Befana said.
"When the rooms are aired and the line dry,
I'll look to the Babe." But the Three rode by.

She worked for a day and a night and a day,
Then, gifts in her hand, took up her way.
But she never could find where the Christ Child lay.
And still she wanders at Christmastide,
Houseless, whose house was all her pride,
Whose heart was tardy, whose gifts were late;
Wanders and knocks at every gate,
Crying, "Good people, the bells begin!
Put off your toiling and let love in!"

AN ANGEL'S MESSAGE

Erma Ferrari

*I*n Jerusalem, where the magi had stopped to inquire for a newly born king, the aged and evil King Herod was alarmed. Was somebody challenging the right of the Herods to rule Judea? "Go and search diligently for the young child," he had told the wise men, "and bring me word, that I may come and worship him also." But the wise men were warned by God of Herod's trickery, and they returned home by another way.

And not long after the magi's visit, Joseph awoke one night from a troubled sleep. "Mary, God spoke to me in a dream, saying, 'Arise, and take the young child and his mother, and flee into Egypt.' We must leave Bethlehem at once, tonight."

Mary quickly gathered some household goods for Joseph to pack on the little donkey. God had spoken to Joseph and she must obey. She did not question the ways of God.

Silently, Joseph led the donkey through the darkness down the southern slope of the city. Beside him, Mary carried the baby.

"When Herod dies, we will return," Joseph said, as they hurried along the caravan route to Egypt.

But Mary and Joseph never returned to Bethlehem. When King Herod died, his equally cruel son, Archelaus, became king of Judea. God directed Joseph to take the young wife and child back to their first home in Nazareth, which lay in Galilee.

And Mary was glad, for in Galilee there were green fields for a growing boy to explore and gentle hills to climb.

Christmas is a quest. May each of us follow his star of faith and find the heart's own Bethlehem.
—*Esther Baldwin York*

The Gift of Glory

*For unto us a
child is born,
unto us a son is
given: and the
government
shall be upon his
shoulder: and
his name shall
be called
Wonderful,
Counsellor, The
mighty God, The
everlasting
Father, The
Prince of Peace.*
—Isaiah 9:6

THE CHRISTMAS STORY

According to the Gospels of Luke and Matthew, KJV

And it came to pass in those days, that there went out a decree from Cæsar Augustus, that all the world should be taxed. And all went to be taxed, every one into his own city. And Joseph also went up from Galilee, out of the city of Nazareth, into Judæa, unto the city of David, which is called Bethlehem; (because he was of the house and lineage of David:) To be taxed with Mary his espoused wife, being great with child.

And so it was, that, while they were there, the days were accomplished that she should be delivered. And she brought forth her firstborn son, and wrapped him in swaddling clothes, and laid him in a manger; because there was no room for them in the inn.

And there were in the same country, shepherds abiding in the field, keeping watch over their flock by night. And lo, the angel of the Lord came upon them, and the glory of the Lord shone round about them: and they were sore afraid. And the angel said unto them, Fear not: for, behold, I bring you good tidings of great joy, which shall be to all people. For unto you is born this day in the city of David a Saviour, which is Christ the Lord. And this shall be a sign unto you; Ye shall find the babe wrapped in swaddling clothes, lying in a manger. And suddenly there was with the angel a multitude of the heavenly host praising God, and saying, Glory to God in the highest, and on earth peace, good will toward men.

And it came to pass, as the angels were gone away from them into heaven, the shepherds said one to another, Let us now go even unto Bethlehem, and see this thing which is come to pass, which the Lord hath made known unto us. And they came with haste, and found Mary, and Joseph, and the babe lying in a manger. And when they had seen it, they made known abroad the saying which was told them concerning this child. And all they that heard it wondered at those things which were told them by the shepherds.

Now when Jesus was born in Bethlehem of Judæa in the days of Herod the king, behold, there came wise men from the east to Jerusalem, saying, Where is he that is born King of the Jews? for we have seen his star in the east, and are come to worship him. When Herod the king had heard these things,

he was troubled, and all Jerusalem with him. And when he had gathered all the chief priests and scribes of the people together, he demanded of them where Christ should be born. And they said unto him, In Bethlehem of Judaea; for thus it is written by the prophet, And thou Bethlehem, in the land of Juda, art not the least among the princes of Juda: for out of thee shall come a Governor, that shall rule my people Israel.

Then Herod, when he had privily called the wise men, inquired of them diligently what time the star appeared. And he sent them to Bethlehem, and said, Go and search diligently for the young child; and when ye have found him, bring me word again, that I may come and worship him also. When they had heard the king, they departed; and lo, the star, which they saw in the east, went before them, till it came and stood over where the young child was. When they saw the star, they rejoiced with exceeding great joy.

And when they were come into the house, they saw the young child with Mary his mother, and fell down and worshiped him: and when they had opened their treasures, they presented unto him gifts: gold, and frankincense and myrrh. And being warned of God in a dream that they should not return to Herod, they departed into their own country another way. And when they

were departed, behold, the angel of the Lord appeareth to Joseph in a dream, saying, Arise, and take the young child and his mother, and flee into Egypt, and be thou there until I bring thee word: for Herod will seek the young child to destroy him. When he arose, he took the young child and his mother by night, and departed into Egypt: And was there until the death of Herod: that it might be fulfilled which was spoken of the Lord by the prophet, saying, Out of Egypt have I called my son.

THE GREATEST GIFT

George Hodges

*N*ow, all that day, travelers had been journeying in unusual numbers along the ways which led to Bethlehem, for it was the time of a census. Caesar Augustus . . . wished to know how many people were living in that part of the country. . . . Every man had to go to his own city; that is, to the place in which his family belonged. So there was a great stir all about the land, with men going to this place and to that to have their names written in the census-books. Among the others, out of Nazareth came Joseph, the carpenter, because he was of the family of David, and with him Mary, his espoused wife, who was to be the mother of the King. Down they came like other poor folk, over hill and dale, till they arrived at Bethlehem. But when they reached the town there was no place where they might stay. Every house was full of guests, and the inn was already crowded. The only shelter was a stable—a common stable, strewn with hay, with dusty cobwebs hanging from the rafters, and occupied by cows and donkeys. There, accordingly, they went.

And there, while the angels sang and the sky blazed over the pastures of the sheep, the King came. The King of Glory came! The mighty God, the Maker of all things, the Lord most high, came to dwell among us. And behold, he was a little child. And Mary wrapped him warm in swaddling clothes, as the way is with babies, and laid him in the manger.

There the shepherds, all out of breath with running, found them—Mary and Joseph, and the babe lying in a manger. And they told what they had seen and heard about the singing angels and the King of Glory while Mary listened, remembering the angel who had appeared to her. So the shepherds returned, glorifying and praising God for all the wonders of that night. Thus was kept the first Christmas, with carols by the choir of heaven, and God's own Son, the Saviour of the world, coming as a Christmas gift for all mankind.

A Mother's Reflection

Kay Hoffman

Sweet little Babe in bed of straw,
Upon thy face I gaze with awe.
You truly are God's own dear Son,
Messiah, the long awaited one.
The shepherds come, Thee to adore
And humbly kneel on straw-strewn floor;

Magi, star-led o'er desert sand,
Have brought Thee jewels from a far land.
The oxen gaze with wondering eyes;

To them You are a sweet surprise.
Gentle doves draw near to coo
Their own soft lullaby to You.

My tiny Babe in bed of straw,
You are the Saviour born for all—
God's gift of love sent from on high.
Sleep, little one, till dawn draws nigh.
The whole world will Thy birth recall,
Messiah born in a stable stall.

Christmas Prayer

Gail Brook Burket

O Prince of Peace, come now to bless
The whole war-weary earth,
As long ago, when angel choirs
Were heralds of Thy birth.

Forgive us when we place our trust
In armament's mad force
And spurn almighty power which stays
The planets in their course.

Give us the will to use our lives
To serve the common good
That all the peoples of the earth
May know true brotherhood.

Oh, let Thy reign supplant the sword
And turn all hearts to Thee.
Thine is the love which conquers all
And Thine true victory.

Celestial choirs from courts above,
Shed sacred glories there;
And angels with their sparkling lyres
Make music on the air.
—*Edmund Hamilton Sears*

MESSIAH

Jim Bishop

The fire outside burned brightly in the southerly breeze. Joseph sat beside it, heating the water and praying. No one came down from the inn to ask how the young woman felt. If she prayed, no one heard except the animals, some of whom stopped chewing for a moment to watch; others of whom opened sleepy eyes to see. The future of mankind hung in space.

Joseph had run out of prayers and promises. He looked up; three stars were fused into one tremendously bright one. His eyes caught the glint of bright blue light, almost like a tiny moon, and he wondered about it and was still vaguely troubled by it when he heard a tiny, thin wail, a sound so slender that one had to listen again for it to make sure. He wanted to rush inside at once. He got to his feet, and he moved no further. She would call him. He would wait.

"Joseph." It was a soft call, but he heard it. At once, he picked up the second jar of water and hurried inside. The two lamps still shed a soft glow over the stable, even though it seemed years since they had been lighted.

The first thing he noticed was his wife. Mary was sitting with her back against a manger wall. Her face was clean; her hair had been brushed. There were blue hollows under her eyes. She smiled at her husband and nodded. She beckoned him to come closer. Joseph, mouth agape, followed her to a little manger. It had been cleaned, but where the animals had nipped the edges of

the wood, the boards were worn and splintered. In the manger were the broad bolts of white swaddling she had brought on the trip. They were doubled underneath and over the top of the baby.

Mary smiled at her husband as he bent far over to look. There, among the cloths, he saw the tiny red face of an infant. This, said Joseph to himself, is the one of whom the angel spoke. He dropped to his knees beside the manger. This was the Messiah.

What Makes Christmas?

Author Unknown

"What is Christmas?"
I asked my soul,
And this answer
Came back to me:
"It is the
Glory of heaven come down
In the hearts of humanity—
Come in the spirit and heart of a Child,
And it matters not what we share
At Christmas; it is not Christmas at all
Unless the Christ Child be there."

The Shepherds Had an Angel

Christina Rossetti

The shepherds had an angel,
The wise men had a star,
But what have I, a little child,
To guide me home from far,
Where glad stars sing together
And singing angels are?

The wise men left their country
To journey morn by morn,
With gold and frankincense and myrrh,
Because the Lord was born;
God sent a star to guide them
And sent a dream to warn.

My life is like their journey,
Their star is like God's book;
I must be like those good wise men

With heavenward heart and look.
But shall I give no gifts to God?
What precious gifts they took!

Lord, I will give my love to Thee,
Than gold much costlier,
Sweeter to Thee than frankincense,
More prized than choicest myrrh.
Lord, make me dearer day by day,
Day by day holier;

Nearer and dearer day by day;
Till I my voice unite
And sing my 'Glory, glory,'
With angels clad in white.
All 'Glory, glory,' given to Thee,
Through all the heavenly height.

THE HOLY NIGHT

Selma Lagerlof

There was a man who went out in the dark night to borrow live coals to kindle a fire. He went from hut to hut and knocked. "Dear friends, help me!" said he. "My wife has just given birth to a child, and I must make a fire to warm her and the little one." But all the people were asleep. No one replied.

The man walked and walked. At last he saw the gleam of a fire a long way off. Then he went in that direction and saw that the fire was burning in the open. A lot of sheep were sleeping around the fire, and an old shepherd sat and watched over the flock.

When the man who wanted to borrow fire came up to the sheep, he saw that three big dogs lay asleep at the shepherd's feet. All three awoke when the man approached and opened their great jaws as though they wanted to bark, but not a sound was heard. The man noticed that the hair on their backs stood up and that their sharp, white teeth glistened in the firelight. They dashed toward him.

One of them bit at his leg and one at his hand and one clung to his throat. But their jaws and teeth wouldn't obey them, and the man didn't suffer harm.

Now the man wished to go farther, to get what he needed. But the sheep lay back to back and so close to one another that he couldn't pass them. Then the man stepped upon their backs and walked over them and up to the fire. And not one of the animals awoke or moved.

When the man had almost reached the fire, the shepherd looked up. He was a surly old man who was unfriendly and harsh toward human beings. And when he saw the strange man coming, he seized the long, spiked staff, which he always held in his hand when he tended his flock, and threw it at him. The staff came right toward the man, but, before it reached him, it turned off to one side and whizzed past him, far out in the meadow.

Now the man came up to the shepherd and said to him: "Good man, help me, and lend me a little fire! My wife has just given birth to a child, and I must make a fire to warm her and the little one."

The shepherd would rather have said no, but when he pondered that the dogs couldn't hurt the man, the sheep had not run from him, and the staff had not wished to strike him, he was afraid and dared not deny the man.

Glory to God in the highest, and peace on earth, goodwill towards men.
—*George F. Handel*

"Take as much as you need!" he said to the man.

But then the fire was nearly burnt out. There were no logs or branches left, only a big heap of live coals; and the stranger had neither spade nor shovel wherein he could carry the red-hot coals.

When the shepherd saw this, he said again: "Take as much as you need!" And he was glad that the man wouldn't be able to take away any coals.

But the man stooped and picked coals from the ashes with his bare hands and laid them in his mantle. And he didn't burn his hands when he touched them, nor did the coals scorch his mantle; but he carried them away as if they had been nuts or apples.

And when the shepherd, who was such a cruel and hardhearted man, saw all this, he began to wonder to himself: What kind of a night is this, when the dogs do not bite, the sheep are not scared, the staff does not kill, or the fire scorch? He called the stranger back and said to him: "What kind of a night is this? And how does it happen that all things show you compassion?"

Then said the man: "I cannot tell you if you do not see it." And he wished to go his way, that he might soon make a fire and warm his wife and child.

But the shepherd did not wish to lose sight of the man before he had found out what all this might portend. He got up and followed the man till they came to the place where he lived.

Then the shepherd saw that the man didn't have so much as a hut to dwell in, but that his wife and babe were lying in a mountain grotto, where there was nothing except the cold and naked stone walls.

But the shepherd thought that perhaps the poor innocent child might freeze to death there in the grotto; and, although he was a hard man, he was touched and thought he would like to help it. And he loosened his knapsack from his shoulder, took from it a soft white sheepskin, gave it to the strange man, and said that he should let the child sleep on it.

But just as soon as he showed that he, too, could be merciful, his eyes were opened, and he saw what he had not been able to see before and heard what he could not have heard before.

He saw that all around him stood a ring of little silver-winged angels, and each held a stringed instrument, and all sang in loud tones that tonight the Saviour was born who should redeem the world from its sins.

Then he understood how all things were so happy this night that they didn't want to do anything wrong.

And it was not only around the shepherd that there were angels, but he saw them everywhere. They sat inside the grotto, they sat outside on the mountain, and they flew under the heavens. They came marching in great companies, and, as they passed, they paused and cast a glance at the child.

There were such jubilation and such gladness and songs and play! And all this he saw in the dark night, whereas before he could not have made out anything. He was so happy because his eyes had been opened that he fell upon his knees and thanked God.

What that shepherd saw we might also see, for the angels fly down from heaven every Christmas Eve, if we could only see them.

You must remember this, for it is as true, as true as that I see you and you see me. It is not revealed by the light of lamps or candles, and it does not depend upon sun and moon; but that which is needful is that we have such eyes as can see God's glory.

As with Gladness Men of Old

William C. Dix

As with gladness men of old
Did the guiding star behold;
As with joy they hailed its light,
Leading onward, beaming bright;
So, most gracious Lord, may we
Evermore your splendor see.

As with joyful steps they sped
To that lowly manger bed,
There to bend the knee before
Christ whom heaven and earth adore;
So may we with hurried pace
Run to seek your throne of grace.

As they offered gifts most rare
At that manger crude and bare;
So may we this holy day,
Drawn to you without delay,
All our costliest treasures bring,
Christ, to you, our heavenly King.

Christ Redeemer, with us stay,
Help us live your holy way;
And when earthly things are past,
Bring our ransomed souls at last
Where they need no star to guide,
Where no clouds your glory hide.

In the heavenly city bright
None shall need created light;
You, its light, its joy, its crown,
You, its sun which goes not down;
There for ever may we sing
Alleluias to our King.

Before the Paling of the Stars

Christina G. Rossetti

Before the paling of the stars,
    Before the winter morn,
Before the earliest cockcrow,
    Jesus Christ was born—
Born in a stable,
    Cradled in a manger,
In the world His hands had made,
    Born a stranger.

Priest and king lay fast asleep
    In Jerusalem;
Young and old lay fast asleep
    In crowded Bethlehem.
Saint and Angel, ox and ass,
    Kept a watch together
Before the Christmas daybreak
    In the winter weather.

Jesus on His mother's breast
    In the stable cold,
Spotless Lamb of God was He,
    Shepherd of the fold.
Let us kneel with Mary maid,
    With Joseph bent and hoary,
With Saint and Angel, ox and ass,
    To hail the King of Glory.

"What is Christmas?" I asked my soul, and this answer came back to me: "It is the glory of heaven come down in the hearts of humanity." —Author Unknown

O Come, All Ye Faithful

JOHN FRANCIS WADE

1. O come, all ye faith - ful, joy - ful and tri - um-phant,
2. Sing, choirs of an - gels, sing in ex - ul - ta - tion!
3. Child, for us sin - ners poor and in the man - ger,
4. Yea, Lord, we greet Thee, born this hap - py morn-ing,

O come ye, O come ye to Beth - le - hem!
O sing, all ye cit - i - zens of heav'n a - bove;
we would em - brace Thee with love and awe;
Je - sus, to Thee be all glo - ry given;

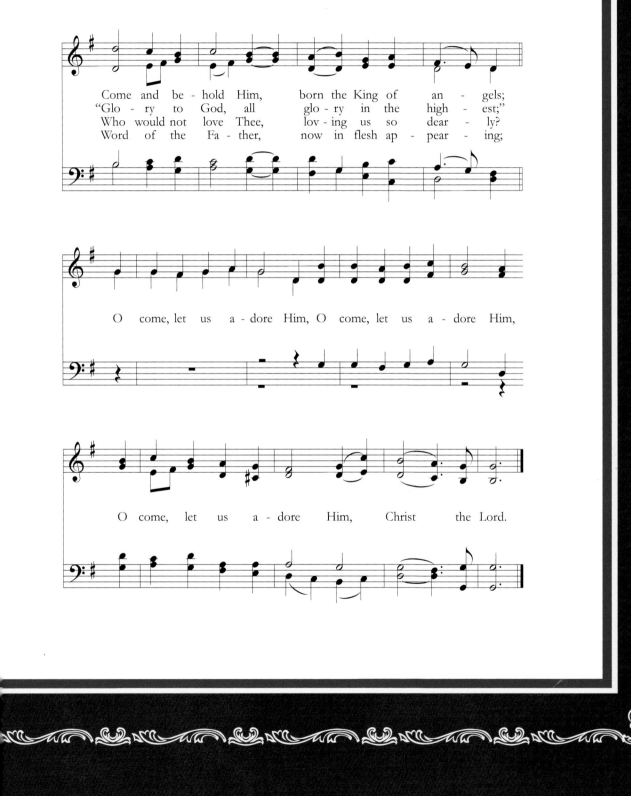

CHRISTMAS ANGEL

Pamela Kennedy

Celestin knew the time was nearing. Not because time mattered to him, but because it was important to Majesty. When the fullness of time arrived, Celestin wanted to be ready to obey instantly. Obedience was the highest service among the angels. It was their never-ending gift to Majesty.

Celestin often pondered the way obedience seemed so difficult for humans. He didn't understand that. Limited as they were by time and space, it seemed only logical that they would want to experience life on earth to the fullest. After all, their days were brief. Couldn't they see that Majesty knew best? He spoke His eternal wisdom to them in nature, whispered it to them through their souls, wrote it in His Word, and shouted it through His prophets. Still they resisted. Now, in an act of grace and mercy Celestin could not comprehend, Majesty was sending the Only Begotten to these stiff-necked creatures. Surely now, they would finally learn obedience and experience the richness of living according to their Maker's will.

It had been almost a year in earth time since Gabriel traveled to Nazareth to speak to Mary. Celestin understood why she had been chosen. He had watched as Gabriel told the young maiden of Majesty's plan. Despite her troubled questions, she had bowed her head in humble obedience and said, "I am the Lord's servant. May it be to me as you have said." Oh, how the angelic choir had rejoiced at that moment! Celestin could still hear the chords of praise echoing in the eternal reaches of heaven.

Celestin wondered how Majesty would introduce the Only Begotten to the world. Perhaps it would be in a mighty temple with row upon row of priests praising God and blowing trumpets. Maybe there would be a tremendous earthquake or tidal wave presaging the event. Majesty used pillars of fire and parted water when he helped Moses, but Celestin felt sure there would be something more magnificent and wonderful for the Only Begotten. He would have to wait and see. Impatience was not becoming of an angel.

When the call came, it was not at all what Celestin had expected. He was to take a multitude of angels and travel to a dark hillside outside a little town called Bethlehem. There he was to make an announcement to a small group of poor men tending a flock of sheep. He was to say: "Do not be afraid. I

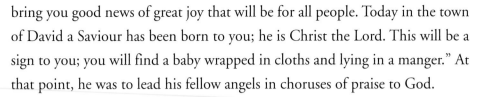

bring you good news of great joy that will be for all people. Today in the town of David a Saviour has been born to you; he is Christ the Lord. This will be a sign to you; you will find a baby wrapped in cloths and lying in a manger." At that point, he was to lead his fellow angels in choruses of praise to God.

"Are you sure that's it?" Celestin asked the messenger from the Throne. "No temple or palace or parted seas or comet shower or anything?"

The other angel shook his head. Then he raised his hand as if remembering something. "Oh, there will be a star," he added.

"A star?" Celestin repeated incredulously. "Just one star?"

"Yes," the messenger repeated with a sigh, "just one star—over a little animal shelter, behind an inn, on a back alley in Bethlehem."

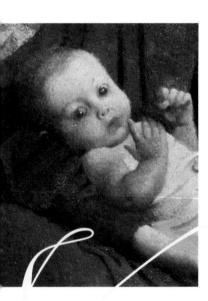

"With all due respect," Celestin continued, "do you think you could have misunderstood the message? We're talking about the Only Begotten here, the Creator, the Sustainer, the Holy One."

The other angel squared his shoulders and looked just a bit perturbed. "That is the message as Majesty gave it to me. I do not question Him." He vanished, leaving Celestin alone and stinging from the mild rebuke.

"Well, I only asked," he muttered. "I wasn't planning to disobey!"

Quickly he summoned a company of angels and led them to the assigned hillside. The shepherds fell on the ground and quaked, just as Celestin had known they would. Humans were always so discomfited by the sight of angels. He reassured them then with Majesty's words and led the angelic choir as they sang, "Glory to God in the highest, and on earth peace to men." He would have preferred something with more hallelujahs, but that wasn't in the orders for tonight.

When the angelic chorus ended and the others returned to heaven, Celestin remained behind. He wanted to see the Only Begotten. He still could not fathom why Majesty had chosen such a homely way to introduce such magnificence.

Silently Celestin hovered in the shadows of the tiny stable. The silver light of one pure star softly illuminated the stony walls. Mary, the obedient one, and Joseph, her loving husband, reclined on the straw. In her arms, she held an infant wrapped in swaddling cloths. Could this be the Only Begotten—here, in these rude surroundings? It was unthinkable. Celestin recalled the dazzling light originating from Majesty's throne, the myriad angels constantly in attendance, the never-ending praises attending His presence. And then he gazed once more at the little family surrounded only by sleeping cows and sheep.

Suddenly, a solitary word flashed into Celestin's mind with brilliant clarity: love. Here in this humble setting, Majesty had spoken it not with thunder or earthquake, nor with an angelic chorus or even a single trumpet blast, but with flesh and blood. The Only Begotten had left the glories of heaven to bring true love to humanity. Here in this tiny town it would begin, but Celestin knew such love could never be confined. Time or space, even eternity, would not be sufficient to contain such abundance. It would flow like a river watering the souls of generation after generation of earth's citizens. A twinge of envy touched Celestin's heart as he realized even an angel could never know such joy as this. He bowed then in reverence before the tiny one lying in Mary's arms, and a gentle breeze brushed the Baby's cheek as the angel whispered, "Holy, Holy, Holy."

The Risk of Birth

Madeleine L'Engle

This is no time for a child to be born,
With the earth betrayed by war and hate
And a nova lighting the sky to warn
That time runs out and sun burns late.

That was no time for a child to be born,
In a land in the crushing grip of Rome;
Honour and truth were trampled by scorn—
Yet here did the Saviour make His home.

When is the time for love to be born?
The inn is full on the planet earth,
And by greed and pride the sky is torn—
Yet Love still takes the risk of birth.

A Christmas Gift
Clarence Hawkes

A Christmas gift Love sends to thee,
'Tis not a gift that you may see,
Like frankincense or shining gold;
Yet 'tis a gift that you may hold.

If you are lacking bread and meat,
'Twill give you heavenly bread to eat;
If you are down-trod, e'en as Job,
'Twill dress you in a seamless robe.

The gift of love in Mary's eyes
Looked down on Jesus with surprise,
That One so great should be so small,
To point the way for kings and all.

One heart of love can move the race;
One grain of truth can change earth's face:
A Bethlehem Babe, a shepherd's rod
Have lifted mankind up to God.

Christmas Day
Philip Doddridgea

Hark, the glad sound! the Saviour comes,
The Saviour promised long;
Let every heart prepare a throne
And every voice a song!

He comes, the broken heart to bind,
The bleeding soul to cure,
And with the treasures of His grace
To enrich the humble poor.

Our glad Hosannas, Prince of Peace,
Thy welcome shall proclaim,
And heaven's eternal arches ring
With Thy beloved name.

TITLE INDEX

AUTHOR INDEX

ACKNOWLEDGMENTS

(continued from page 4) BISHOP, JIM. "Messiah" from *The Day Christ Was Born.* Copyright © 1960 by Jim Bishop and renewed 1988 by Betty Kelly Bishop. Reprinted by permission of HarperCollins Publishers, Inc. BRUN, MARCEL and BOWEN, BETTY. "The Tailor's Christmas Guest" from *The Shining Tree and Other Christmas Stories,* edited by Hildegard Hawthorne and Marcel Brun. Copyright © 1940. DREDLA, ALBERTA. "Christmas Gifts." Used by permission of the author. EVANS, COLLEEN TOWNSEND. "What Shall We Do This Christmas?" from *The Meaning of Christmas.* Edited by Phyllis Hobe. Copyright © 1975 by the editor. Published by A. J. Holman Co./J. B. Lippincott/HarperCollins. FERRARI, ERMA. "An Angel's Message" from *The Life of Jesus of Nazareth* by Erma Ferrari. Copyright © 1958 by Simon and Schuster, Inc. and Artists and Writers Guild, Inc. GUEST, EDGAR A. "A Kindled Flame of Love." Used by permission of Henry Sobell, Jr. HAZELTINE, ALICE ISABEL. "Christmas Roses" from *The Christmas Book of Legends and Stories* by Elva Sophronia Smith and Alice Isabel Hazeltine. Copyright © 1944 by Lothrop, Lee and Shepherd, Co., NY. L'ENGLE, MADELINE. "The Risk of Birth" from *A Treasury of Christmas Classics.* Copyright © 1994 by Harold Shaw Publishers, Wheaton, IL. LEE, LAURIE. "Carols in the Cotswolds" from *The Edge of Day.* Reprinted by permission of United Agents on belalf of The Estate of Laurie Lee. LERNET-HOLENIA, ALEXANDER. "The Three Wise Men of Totenleben," translated by Judith Bernays Heller, from *Christmas Is Here.* Edited by Anne Fremantle. Copyright © 1955 by the Stephen Daye Press. LOGAN, BEN. "The Year the Presents Didn't Come" from *Christmas Remembered.* Copyright © 1997 by Ben Logan. Published by NorthWord Press. MCGINLEY, PHYLLIS. "The Ballad of Befana." Copyright © 1957 by Phyllis McGinley. Reprinted by permission of Curtis Brown Ltd. SMALL, MARY. "Christmas and Peter Moss" from *Star of Wonder: Christmas Stories and Poems for Children.* Collected by Pat Alexander. Copyright © 1996 by Pat Alexander. Lion Publishing, London. Our sincere thanks to the following authors whom we were unable to locate: Heywood Broun for "We Too, Are Bidden"; Mary Ellen Chase for "Late for Christmas"; The Estate of Ralph Spaulding Cushman for "Christmas Prayer"; Clarence Hawkes for "A Christmas Gift"; Pat Corrick Hinton for "Prayer at Christmas"; The Estate of William P. Remington for "The Keeper of the Inn."

PHOTOGRAPHS

Cover, Snow-covered trees in Willard Brook State Forest, Townsend, Massachusetts, © William Johnson; 1-2 Beached glacial ice in Muir Inlet, Glacier Bay National Park, Alaska, © Carr Clifton; 4-5 Sunset over the Teton Range, Grand Teton National Park, Wyoming, © Carr Clifton; 6-7 Snow on the banks of the Ammonoosuc River at sunrise over Twin Mountain, Bethlehem, New Hampshire, © William H. Johnson; 8-9 Antique musical instruments and candles, © Jessie Walker; 11 Homemade holiday treats, © Jessie Walker; 12-13 Cottage decorated for Christmas, © Jessie Walker; 14-15 *WIND CHILL* by Karl J. Kuerner III, © Superstock; 18-19 *SCHOOL'S OUT* by Samuel S. Carr, © Christie's Images/Bridgeman Art Library; 22 Door decorated for Christmas, © Jessie Walker; 26 Lighted log cottages in Colorado snow, © Superstock; 29 Snow-covered hill in Maine, © Superstock; 30-31 Snowy trees and field, © Superstock; 32-33 *UNTRODDEN SNOW WITHIN THREE MILES OF CHARING CROSS, HOLLAND PARK* by Andrew McCallum © Christie's Images/Bridgeman Art Library; 34-35 *A DUTCH VILLAGE IN WINTER* by Willem Koekkoek, © Christie's Images/SuperStock; 38-39 *GOING TO CHURCH* by Hermann Kaufmann, © Christie's Image/SuperStock; 41 *A PORTRAIT OF A GIRL IN A WINTER LANDSCAPE* by Harry Van Der Weyden, © Christie's Images/Bridgeman Art Library; 44-45 *A CAPRICCO VIEW OF A TOWN WITH FIGURES ON A FROZEN CANAL* by Jan Hendrik Verheyen, © Christie's Images/Bridgeman Art Library; 49 *L'HIVER A MOUTON CAULT* by Camille Pissarro, © Christie's Images/SuperStock; 50 Baskets of vegetables on table with candles, © Jessie Walker; 52-53 Sun streaming through snow-covered trees, © Superstock; 54 *L'EGLISE DE JEUFOSSE, TEMPS DE NEIGE* by Claude Monet, © Christie's Images/Bridgeman Art Library; 57 Snow-covered fir tree with lights and ornaments at dusk in Bristol, New Hampshire, © William H. Johnson; 58-59 *NURSEMAIDS, HIGH BRIDGE PARK* by George Luks, © Christie's Images/Bridgeman Art Library; 63 *THE CHRISTMAS TREE* by Elizabeth Adela Stanhope, © Christie's Images/SuperStock; 67 Lighted church at dusk in a New England Town, © Superstock; 68-69 *MILLSTREAM IN NEW EPSWICH, NEW HAMPSHIRE* by William Jurian Kaula, © Superstock; 72-73 Antique Christmas card, © Fine Art Photographic Library Ltd.; 74-75 Winter sun in the Shawangunk Mountains of New York, © Carr Clifton; 76-77 Peaks above Saint Mary Lake, Glacier National Park, Montana, © Carr Clifton; 78 Snow-covered fir trees on Old Speck Mountain, Grafton Notch State Park, Maine, © William H. Johnson; 80-81 *TIMES SQUARE, WINTER IN NEW YORK* by Guy Carleton Wiggins, © Christie's Images/Bridgeman Art Library; 84-85 Winter landscape in North Kingstown, Rhode Island, © Superstock; 86-87 *WINTER LANDSCAPE WITH A CHURCH* by Caspar David Friedrich, © Christie's Images/Bridgeman Art Library; 90-91 *CHRISTMAS CHEER* by George Sheridan Knowles, © Christie's Images/Fine Art Photographic Library, London; 94-95 *TWILIGHT IN GLOUCESTER* by Paul Cornoyer, © Christie's Images/SuperStock; 96-97 Fir tree in the snow decorated for the season, © William H. Johnson; 98-99 Snow-covered trees on a sunny winter day, © Superstock; 100-101 Christmas tree decorated with apples and cookies, © Jessie Walker; 103 Winter landscape at sunset, © Superstock; 104-105 Sunset on Saint Mary Lake, Glacier National Park, Montana, © Carr Clifton; 107 Sunrise over Cape Hatteras National Seashore, North Carolina, © Carr Clifton; 108 *MUSIC-MAKING ANGEL WITH LUTE* by Melozzo da Forli, © Superstock; 111 *THE WINTER SHEPHERD* by Daniel Sherrin, © Fine Art Photographic Library Ltd.; 114-115 *ADORATION OF THE SHEPHERDS* by Francesco Zuccarelli, © Superstock; 119 Two angels by Unknown Artist, © Fine Arts Photographic Library Ltd.; 120-121 *ADORATION OF THE SHEPHERDS* by Louis Le Nain, © Superstock; 122-123 *THE NATIVITY* by Gari Melchers, © Superstock; 124-125 *A FROZEN WINTER LANDSCAPE* by Johannes Bartholomaus Duntze, © Christie's Images/CORBIS; 127 *TOBIOLO AND THE ANGEL* detail by Giovanni Girolamo Savoldo, © Superstock; 128-129 Hemlock tree trunks covered with snow at sunrise, Wompatuck State Park, Massachusetts, © William H. Johnson; 130-131 *AN ANGEL* by John Melhuish Strudwick, © Christie's Images/Bridgeman Art Library; 132-133 *FLIGHT INTO EGYPT* by Gysbrecht Leytens, © Fine Art Photographic Library Ltd.; 134 *ADORATION OF THE SHEPHERDS* by Domenico Zampieri Domenichino, © Fine Art Photographic Library Ltd.; 136-137 *THE BIRTH OF CHRIST* by Abraham Bloomaert, © Superstock; 138-139 *THE MADONNA AND CHILD IN GLORY WITH CHERUBS* by Giovanni Battista Salvi, il Sassoferrato, © Christie's Images/Bridgeman Art Library; 141 Sunset over the Androscoggin River Valley, Bethel, Maine, © William H. Johnson; 144-145 *THE HOLY FAMILY* by Luca Giordano, © Fine Art Photographic Library Ltd.; 146-147 *THE ADORATION OF THE SHEPHERDS* attributed to Willem Van Herp, © Christie's Images/Bridgeman Art Library; 148 The Pemigewasset River and Falls in Franconia Notch State Park, New Hampshire, © William H. Johnson; 152 *ANGELS AND HOLY CHILD* by Marianne Stokes, © Fine Art Photographic Library Ltd.; 156-157 Snow-capped peaks of the Grand Tetons, Montana, © Terry Donnelly.